A GIFT FOR YOU

D1250065

WHAT IS LIFE ABOUT?

THE LIFE BOOK

By Carl Blunt

twitter.com/carlblunt
facebook.com/carlblunt

Written by Carl Blunt
twitter.com/carlblunt
facebook.com/carlblunt

For more information on The Life Book Project please go to:
www.thelifebook.com

The Life Book Project exists to put God's Word in the hands and hearts of
every high school student.

Fifth Printing.

WHAT IS THE LIFE BOOK?

PART 1

Part 1 is God's story before Jesus shows up on the scene. It's a quick re-telling of the first part of the Bible before Jesus arrives. It explains how things were great, then went bad and why Jesus has to come make things right.

PART 2

Part 2 is straight from the Bible. It's the story of Jesus while He was on Earth. He does some amazing stuff.

WHAT ABOUT YOU?

This part is about what God's story means for your life. What does Jesus have to do with you? What is your role in the world God created? What does God want from you?

HELP!

This part gives some help and answers for things you or your friends might be struggling with. The Bible is full of good answers and guidance for tough stuff in life. It's God's advice, so it has to be pretty good.

STUDENT NOTES

Four students make notes and ask questions all through The Life Book.
(Free Clue: You can tell each student apart by their handwriting.)

DYLAN

I'm 17. Not really into spiritual stuff, but open-minded. Love gaming and science fiction. When I graduate, I want to design the first mass produced flying car.

I hate it when people are fake. I love asking questions and trying to figure things out. My dog's name is Buster. I spend most of my time hanging with Jake Foster doing stupid stuff.

TAYLOR (TAY)

15 yrs old. I'm just a girl who loves God and hope you do too! I want to help others learn more about Jesus. Maybe be a missionary or something like that, so I can tell others how much God loves them. I hope my notes help you. I love helping people and hate it when people are mean.

I play guitar, piano and sing but I'm not sure if I'm any good.

PEDRO (A.K.A. PB)

Freshman this year. Friends call me PB because I put peanut butter on everything. Love sports and am pretty good at them. Hope to play professional football when I get older. Still trying to figure out God and stuff. My girlfriend tells me about Him.

Moved to a new school this year. Hope to start at quarterback. I hate sitting on the bench. I don't get people who don't like sports.

Spend a lot of time with my girlfriend. I pretty much hate homework.

VANESSA

Just turned 16. Love guys. Wish life wasn't so messed up.
I want to be a singer someday. Go to church every week, but it's not
a big deal, just something mom and I do together.
Kinda interested in what God is all about. Hate it when people talk about
me behind my back. Love knowing all the gossip.
Dream a lot. Just waiting for the man of my dreams to become real.

ADULT NOTES

UNCLE G. (A.K.A. GIDEON WILLIAMS)

I'm the old guy, but I love God and love teens. Those who know me call me Uncle G.
I grew up in the 'hood' as they call it. Thanks to my mom I made it through.
And thanks to my grandma, I became a follower of Jesus. I'm just here to put in
my two cents.

I still don't understand everything about God and the Bible, but I hope I can help
a little bit. They say my gray hair gives me wisdom. I don't know about that, but I
do know that I've tried to learn as much as I can through the years. So, I hope I
can help you get to know God and Jesus better.

PART 1

THE STORY OF GOD AND PEOPLE
(quick retelling of the first part of the Bible)

GOD MAKES IT ALL

(read more in Genesis, the first book in the Bible)

Before time began (as we know it), God existed. That seems tough to understand, but God was and is and will always be. I guess when you are God, you don't have to explain it all.

I want that kind of power -D

As God, He didn't need to make anything, but He decided to make the universe and put people on earth. He spoke and everything was created. No magic, no illusions, just a word followed by a world.

IT'S ALL GOOD

(read more in Genesis Chapter 2)

In the Bible, God says that everything He made was good. From massive galaxies soaked with shiny stars to tiny molecules packed with DNA, it was all good. As part of creating our world, God made a man named Adam and a woman named Eve. What is really cool is that the Bible says God made them in His image. We don't know exactly what God looks like because the Bible says He is a spirit, but we do know that He made humans in His likeness. God has the power to create and He made us creative too. Being made in His image, we also have the power to love and reason, dream and desire.

I really wish everything was still ALL good. Things are pretty messed up. -V

It's pretty cool when you think about it. We may not be all-wise, all-powerful, and perfect in every way, but God did make us like Him in some ways. God is not just some uncaring ruler who runs things from a distance, blessing and punishing people. He actually cares about the people He made.

Cool thought. -PB

In the Garden of Eden where God placed Adam and Eve, there was no death or suffering, no sin or sadness. Complete trust of each other and God brought pure joy to every moment. God gave them everything they needed and it was a perfect relationship. They were free to do anything except eat the fruit from one special tree.

Can't imagine -PB

EVIL VILLAIN SHOWS UP

(read more in Genesis Chapter 3)

Totally hate snakes! - Tay

Snakes can't be trusted. Satan (an angel who was kicked out of heaven when he tried to take over) basically told Adam and Eve that God was lying to them and that they shouldn't trust Him. Satan told them that God didn't want them eating from the special tree because He was just trying to keep them from becoming like Him. He also told them God was bluffing on the punishment, which was death.

I know what it's like to make bad choices when it comes to trust. –V

Adam and Eve thought it over, trashed their trust of God, chose to trust the snake Satan and took a bite that would change the world. In that one bite, trust was shattered, and the relationship between God and Adam and Eve was broken. As a result, evil (sin) entered into the perfect world.

Really? One bite and the whole human race has to pay? -J

THE CURSE

A curse fell on Adam and Eve as well as all who would come after them. Now the perfect world would be messy and full of struggle, pain, suffering and shame. Because of their sin, death entered the world. Plants, animals, Adam and Eve, and all their offspring would live for a while and then die. There was no longer the possibility of a close relationship with God. He had to kick them out of the perfect Garden of Eden, and He would no longer walk with them, talk with them, or be close with them as He had before. Sin was now between them.

> *Just never thought of my sin and stuff as a big deal.*
> *-PB*

MURDER

The curse of sin and evil in the world showed its ugly head when Adam and Eve's son Cain killed his brother Abel. For many, many years, evil ruled on the earth until God decided it was time to start over.

DO-OVER

God found one man who was living right and chose him to start everything all over. He asked Noah to build a huge boat that would survive a world-wide flood. In this huge boat, Noah took his family and a pair of each animal so they could repopulate the earth.

Glad I wasn't Noah. Build a boat in the desert? No way. -V

The flood came and the world was wiped out, except for the people and the animals on the huge boat. They started over.

STARTING AGAIN

Because the flood did not break the curse, sin and rebellion against God's ways started all over again. God started a new nation by making a huge promise to

His chosen leader named Abraham. He told Abraham that he would be the father of many nations. Oh, by the way, Abraham and his wife Sarah <u>were</u> really old when God made this promise.

I remember this part of the Bible. Sarah laughed when Abraham told her. — Tay

I saw the Joseph musical on Broadway with my aunt. Didn't he have a colored coat or something like that? — V

Eventually Isaac (Abraham and Sarah's son) was born and became a leader of God's people. Isaac had a son named Jacob (who was quite a schemer). Jacob moved his family to Egypt to escape a famine and eventually had a son named Joseph, who stayed faithful to God even though he went through a bunch of bad stuff like slavery and prison. God eventually used him to save His family.

Science check. Okay, how does that happen? On fire, but not burning? I guess if you believe God made everything, then He can mess with scientific laws whenever he wants. — D

SLAVERY

For about 400 years, God's people lived as slaves in Egypt. Until . . . God lit up a bush in the desert. God signed up Moses as the next leader by speaking to him through a burning bush (the bush was on fire, but not burning up in the desert.

Plague = bad stuff! Water turning to blood, frogs everywhere. disease. locusts. darkness. etc. Bad stuff! — Tay

Moses asked Pharaoh to set God's people free from slavery. Pharaoh refused and God sent a nasty <u>plague.</u> Moses kept asking — Pharaoh kept refusing — God kept sending plagues on Egypt. You'd think Pharaoh would get the message. One final request, one final denial and then God sent the worst plague of all.

Glad he wasn't leading my country. — PB

PASSING OVER

Before God sent the last plague (death of the firstborn from every family), He gave Moses some specific directions to save the lives of His people. (God seems

to always provide a way to be saved from terrible <u>consequences</u>.) God told
Moses to have each family kill a lamb and smear the lamb's blood over the top
of the door to their house.

True!
— Tay

When the plague came, all of God's people were saved but the firstborn of each
Egyptian family died. Pharaoh gave in and decided to set God's people free.

That's really sad. Seems unfair for the Egyptians to die
just because Pharaoh was a jerk. — V

They took off only to have Pharaoh change his mind and follow them. With the
Red Sea in front of them and Pharaoh's army behind them, God miraculously
parted the sea. God's people crossed over, the sea moved back into place and
they finally tasted freedom.

And Pharaoh's army drowned — saw part
of the movie. — PB

10 LAWS

Free from slavery, God gave Moses 10 laws that would help His people live in
such a way that God would be honored and their society would work. The laws
were not given to punish them, but every law had a good purpose to help God's
people live together well and have a relationship with God.

Never thought about God's laws
like that. — V

Some of the laws were about not worshipping <u>idols</u>, not stealing, lying, and
stuff like that.

I think maybe we still turn to idols. Forgive me. — Tay

Instead of following the ten commandments, many of God's people turned to
idols and other gods. Because the curse was still in effect, people also ignored

some of the other laws. God's laws didn't break the curse, but when people broke His laws, it was just more evidence that the curse was real and it was strong.

BLOOD PAYMENT

Unfortunately, the laws were broken often. So God gave His people a plan to pay for their law breaking. Because blood is the source of life for all, God's plan for payment involved the spilling of blood (kind of like when He protected His people from the final plague in Egypt).

Animals were to be sacrificed as payment for sin and wrong doing. The curse could not be broken by these sacrifices, but the blood of an animal would provide temporary cover from God's punishment of their sin.

Kind of weird to think that blood somehow made up for sin. I guess it makes more sense of Jesus being killed. — PB

I know it sounds strange, but I sometimes feel the pull of this curse — V

The curse still reigned in the world — the curse that entered the world because of Adam and Eve's decision to choose to trust Satan instead of God still reigned in the world.

THE PROMISE

Through His people, God began to share the promise of one who would come and break the curse once and for all. A Messiah, a leader, a Savior was coming who would fix the relationship between humans and God. This Savior would not only show us a new way to live, but He would also be the final sacrifice — his blood paying the penalty for all sin.

Remember: sin equals death and the Bible refers to death as hell (being punished forever). Someone would have to pay for our sin. Without a Savior, the result of our sin is eternal punishment.* You might say we were on a highway to hell. The promised Savior would provide us a way to avoid being punished forever.

Handwritten margin note: Oh, so he took our place? – PB

Handwritten note: *Yes! – Uncle G

Handwritten note: Amazing when I think about it. Thank you Jesus for breaking the curse. – Tay

The blood of animals covered sin before Jesus showed up, but the only way to finally break the curse once and for all was to have a perfect sacrifice. According to those who told about His coming, the promised Savior would live a life without any sin. He would be absolutely perfect. But in a strange twist of events, He would offer His innocent life and pure blood as a final sacrifice by allowing people to kill Him. His blood would pay the penalty for all sin.

Handwritten note: So that's why Jesus died? I had no idea –D

THE HOPE

When the Savior comes, all who chose to believe (trust) that His final sacrifice really did break the curse, would have the curse broken in their own life.* They would be made right with God and all of their sin would be forgiven. They would become followers of this Savior, living like He lived and helping others come to trust in His ways.

Handwritten note: See my note on the next page.

JESUS CHRIST SHOWS UP

Part 2 is all about the promised one, Jesus Christ, showing up. Jesus comes as the eternal Son of God in human form to forever break the curse. He was fully divine and fully human. His own people (God's chosen people) rejected Him, yet He lived a pure life without sin, and because of this, he became the perfect sacrifice. He took our place, spilling His own blood as the final sacrifice to break the curse. Miraculously proving He was God's eternal son, God raised Him from the dead.

Here is the true story of Jesus that forever changed the world and just maybe your life . . .

*That's what it was like for me. I was sixteen and headed the wrong way when some older guy gave me a little green Bible in the detention center. I read it because I didn't have anything else to do and he seemed different, like he actually cared about me. I didn't understand a lot of what the Bible said, but I did realize that I was messed up and needed a new start. There was a section in the back that talked about being forgiven and following Jesus. I prayed the prayer they had in there and my life began to change. Not sure what happened except that God got hold of me and started making changes. I wish I could find the guy who gave me that Bible and thank him. Because of him my sins are forgiven, I am living the life God wants for me and I am going to heaven when I die.

- Uncle G.

PART 2

THE STORY OF JESUS COMING TO EARTH
(The REAL Bible as God gave it to us)

BOOK OF JOHN
(straight from the Bible)

In the beginning was the Word, and the Word was with God, and the Word
was God. He was with God in the beginning. All things were created through Him,
and apart from Him not one thing was created that has been created. Life was
in Him, and that life was the light of men. That light shines in the darkness, yet
the darkness did not overcome it.

There was a man named John who was sent from God. He came as a witness
to testify about the light, so that all might believe through him. He was not
the light, but he came to testify about the light.

The true light, who gives light to everyone, was coming into the world.
He was in the world, and the world was created through Him, yet the
world did not recognize Him. He came to His own, and His own people
did not receive Him. But to all who did receive Him, He gave them the right to be
children of God, to those who believe in His name, who were born, not of blood,
or of the will of the flesh, or of the will of man, but of God.

The Word became flesh and took up residence among us. We observed
His glory, the glory as the One and Only Son from the Father, full of grace
and truth. (John testified concerning Him and exclaimed, "This was the One
of whom I said, 'The One coming after me has surpassed me, because He
existed before me.'") Indeed, we have all received grace after grace from His
fullness, for although the law was given through Moses, grace and truth came

through Jesus Christ. No one has ever seen God. The One and Only Son — the One who is at the Father's side — He has revealed Him.

John the Baptist's Testimony

This is John's testimony when the Jews from Jerusalem sent priests and Levites to ask him, "Who are you?" He did not refuse to answer, but he declared: "I am not the Messiah." "What then?" they asked him. "Are you Elijah?" "I am not," he said. "Are you the Prophet?" "No," he answered. "Who are you, then?" they asked. "We need to give an answer to those who sent us. What can you tell us about yourself?"

Man, they are drilling the guy. - D

Felt like that before, except no one was listening. - Tay

He said, "I am a voice of one crying out in the <u>wilderness</u>: Make straight the way of the Lord just as Isaiah the prophet said." Now they had been sent from the Pharisees. So they asked him, "Why then do you baptize if you aren't the Messiah, or Elijah, or the Prophet?"

Not sure I get the whole baptism thing. - PB

"I baptize with water," John answered them. "Someone stands among you, but you don't know Him. He is the One coming after me, whose sandal strap I'm not worthy to untie." All this happened in Bethany across the Jordan, where John was baptizing. *

* When I was just a boy, momma would give me a bath every night because I would get all dirty playing in the abandoned lot next to where we lived. Every night she would tell me about how water makes us new and fresh again. No matter how dirty I got, she always made me clean. So baptism reminds me of that. - Uncle G.

The Lamb of God

The next day John saw Jesus coming toward him and said, "Here is the Lamb of God, who takes away the sin of the world! This is the One I told you about: 'After me comes a man who has surpassed me, because He existed before me.' I didn't know Him, but I came baptizing with water so He might be revealed to Israel."

That would be cool to see. People probably freaked. – V

And John testified, "I watched the Spirit descending from heaven like a dove, and He rested on Him. I didn't know Him, but He who sent me to baptize with water told me, 'The One you see the Spirit descending and resting on—He is the One who baptizes with the Holy Spirit.' I have seen and testified that He is the Son of God!"

Again the next day, John was standing with two of his disciples. When he saw Jesus passing by, he said, "Look! The Lamb of God!" The two disciples heard him say this and followed Jesus. When Jesus turned and noticed them following Him, He asked them, "What are you looking _for?_" They said to Him, "Rabbi" (which means "Teacher"), "where are You staying?" "Come and you'll see," He replied. So they went and saw where He was staying, and they stayed with Him that day. It was about 10 in the morning.

Jesus loves to ask lots of ????s. – Tay

Andrew, Simon Peter's brother, was one of the two who heard John and followed Him. He first found his own brother Simon and told him, "We have found the Messiah!" (which means "Anointed One"), and he brought Simon to Jesus. When Jesus saw him, He said, "You are Simon, son of John. You will be called Cephas" (which means "Rock").

Wonder what name Jesus would give me? – V

Philip and Nathanael

The next day He decided to leave for Galilee. Jesus found Philip and told him, "Follow Me!" Now Philip was from Bethsaida, the hometown of Andrew and Peter. Philip found Nathanael and told him, "We have found the One Moses wrote about in the Law (and so did the prophets): Jesus the son of Joseph, from Nazareth!" "Can anything good come out of Nazareth?" Nathanael asked him. "Come and see," Philip answered. Then Jesus saw Nathanael coming toward Him and said about him, "Here is a true Israelite; no deceit is in him." "How do you know me?" Nathanael asked. "Before Philip called you, when you were under the fig tree, I saw you," Jesus answered. "Rabbi," Nathanael replied, "You are the Son of God! You are the King of Israel!" Jesus responded to him, "Do you believe [only] because I told you I saw you under the fig tree? You will see greater things than this." Then He said, "I assure you: You will see heaven opened and the angels of God ascending and descending on the Son of Man."

[handwritten margin note:] Are you stalking me? LOL - D

CHAPTER 2

The First Sign: Turning Water into Wine

On the third day a wedding took place in Cana of Galilee. Jesus' mother was there, and Jesus and His disciples were invited to the wedding as well. When the wine ran out, Jesus' mother told Him, "They don't have any wine." "What has this concern of yours to do with Me, woman?" Jesus asked. "My hour has not yet come." "Do whatever He tells you," His mother told the servants. Now six stone water jars had been set there for Jewish purification. Each contained 20 or 30 gallons. "Fill the jars with water," Jesus told them. So they filled them to the brim. Then He said to them, "Now draw some out and take it to the chief servant." And they did. When the chief servant tasted the water (after it had become wine), he did not know where it came from—though the servants who had drawn the water knew. He called the groom and told him, "Everybody sets out the fine wine first, then, after people have drunk freely, the inferior. But you have kept the fine wine until now." Jesus performed this first sign in Cana of Galilee. He displayed His glory, and His disciples believed in Him. After this, He went down to Capernaum, together with His mother, His brothers, and His disciples, and they stayed there only a few days.

→ Okay, let me get this straight: 1. Jesus is at a party 2. He is making wine. Hmmm... totally different than the Jesus I've heard about. K. Got me thinking. - PB

Cleansing the Temple Complex

The Jewish Passover was near, so Jesus went up to Jerusalem. In the temple complex He found people selling oxen, sheep, and doves, and [He also found] the money changers sitting there. After making a whip out of cords, He drove everyone out of the temple complex with their sheep and oxen. He also poured out the money changers' coins and overturned the tables. He told those who were selling doves,

Cool. Never knew Jesus got ticked off. So much for the meek little teacher. - D

"Get these things out of here! Stop turning My Father's house into a marketplace!" And His disciples remembered that it is written: Zeal for Your house will consume Me.

So the Jews replied to Him, "What sign [of authority] will You show us for doing these things?" Jesus answered, "Destroy this sanctuary, and I will raise it up in three days." Therefore the Jews said, "This sanctuary took 46 years to build, and will You raise it up in three days?" But He was speaking about the sanctuary of His body. So when He was raised from the dead, His disciples remembered that He had said this. And they believed the Scripture and the statement Jesus had made. While He was in Jerusalem at the Passover Festival, many trusted in His

Jesus seems to confuse people a lot. - V

Wish all my friends and family would start to trust in Jesus. - Tay

name when they saw the signs He was doing. Jesus, however, would not entrust Himself to them, since He knew them all and because He did not need anyone to testify about man; for He Himself knew what was in man.

CHAPTER 3

Jesus and Nicodemus

There was a man from the Pharisees named Nicodemus, a ruler of the Jews. This man came to Him at (night) and said, "Rabbi, we know that You have come from God as a teacher, for no one could perform these signs You do unless God were with him."

Wonder what it's like sneaking around at night in one of those robe things. Funny. – D

Jesus replied, "I assure you: Unless someone is born again, he cannot see the kingdom of God."

I definitely want to see the kingdom of God! – Tay

"But how can anyone be born when he is old?" Nicodemus asked Him. "Can he enter his mother's womb a second time and be born?"

Don't even want to think about that. – V

Jesus answered, "I assure you: Unless someone is born of water and the Spirit, he cannot enter the kingdom of God. Whatever is born of the flesh is flesh, and whatever is born of the Spirit is spirit. Do not be amazed that I told you that you must be born again. The wind blows where it pleases, and you hear its sound, but you don't know where it comes from or where it is going. So it is with everyone born of the Spirit."

"How can these things be?" asked Nicodemus.

I'm with you Nic. I'd be asking the same thing! – PB

"Are you a teacher of Israel and don't know these things?" Jesus replied. "I assure you: We speak what We know and We testify to what We have seen, but you do not accept Our testimony. If I have told you about things that happen on Earth and you don't believe, how will you believe if I tell you about things of heaven? No one has ascended into heaven except the One who descended from heaven — the Son of Man. Just as Moses lifted up the snake in the wilderness, so the Son of Man must be lifted up, so that everyone who believes in Him will have eternal life."

Snakes again? – Tay

For God loved the world in this way: He gave His One and Only Son, so that everyone who believes in Him will not perish but have eternal life.

Saw a guy at a pro football game with a big sign that said this. – PB

For God did not send His Son into the world that He might condemn the world, but that the world might be saved through Him. Anyone who believes in Him is not condemned, but anyone who does not believe is already condemned, because he has not believed in the name of the One and Only Son of God.

I didn't know that. Condemned already for not believing? Does that mean I'm going to hell if I don't believe in Jesus? – D

This, then, is the judgment: the light has come into the world, and people loved darkness rather than the light because their deeds were evil. For everyone who practices wicked things hates the light and avoids it, so that his deeds may not be exposed. But anyone who lives by the truth comes to the light, so that his works may be shown to be accomplished by God.

I know people like that. – V

*Hell? Jesus talks a whole bunch about it. Did Jesus just make it up to scare people? No, it's real. It may seem unfair to be condemned already (on a highway to hell) for not believing, but we all deserve it because we rebel against God by doing our own thing and breaking His rules. We are all born with the curse of sin. The result of that curse is hell - punishment forever. Everyone who does not believe in who Jesus is and what He has done for them will experience the lake of fire Jesus talks about. BUT - don't forget - God provides a way to be with Him forever in heaven. Believe in Jesus just like He said. So, I guess the most loving thing I can do for you is tell you how you can avoid hell and spend forever in heaven.

- Uncle G.

Jesus and John the Baptist

After this, Jesus and His disciples went to the Judean countryside, where He spent time with them and baptized. John also was baptizing in Aenon near Salim, because there was plenty of water there. People were coming and being baptized, since John had not yet been thrown into prison. Then a dispute arose between John's disciples and a Jew about purification. So they came to John and told him, "Rabbi, the One you testified about, and who was with you across the Jordan, is baptizing—and everyone is flocking to Him." John responded, "No one can receive a single thing unless it's given to him from heaven. You yourselves can testify that I said, 'I am not the Messiah, but I've been sent ahead of Him.' He who has the bride is the groom. But the groom's friend, who stands by and listens for him, rejoices greatly at the groom's voice. So this joy of mine is complete. He must increase, but I must decrease."

Prison? Must be coming up. - PB

Decrease? I guess it means God gets more attention and I get less? Honestly that's a tough thing for me I love attention - V

The One from Heaven

The One who comes from above is above all. The one who is from the earth is earthly and speaks in earthly terms. The One who comes from heaven is above all. He testifies to what He has seen and heard, yet no one accepts His testimony. The one who has accepted His testimony has affirmed that God is true. For God sent Him, and He speaks God's words, since He gives the Spirit without measure. The Father loves the Son and has given all things into His hands. The one who believes in the Son has eternal life, but the one who refuses to believe in the Son will not see life; instead, the wrath of God remains on him.

There it is again— don't believe = punishment. Hmmm - D

CHAPTER 4

Jesus and the Samaritan Woman

When Jesus knew that the Pharisees heard He was making and baptizing more disciples than John (though Jesus Himself was not baptizing, but His disciples were), He left Judea and went again to Galilee. He had to travel through Samaria, so He came to a town of Samaria called Sychar near the property that Jacob had given his son Joseph. Jacob's well was there, and Jesus, worn out from His journey, sat down at the well. It was about six in the evening. A woman of Samaria came to draw water. "Give Me a drink," Jesus said to her, for His disciples had gone into town to buy food. "How is it that You, a Jew, ask for a drink from me, a Samaritan woman?" she asked Him. For Jews do not associate with Samaritans. *Jesus doesn't seem to care about stupid rules. I like that. - PB*

Living water? - V

Jesus answered, "If you knew the gift of God, and who is saying to you, 'Give Me a drink,' you would ask Him, and He would give you living water." "Sir," said the woman, "You don't even have a bucket, and the well is deep. So where do you get this 'living water'? You aren't greater than our father Jacob, are you? He gave us the well and drank from it himself, as did his sons and livestock."

Now it makes sense. Living water means eternal life. - V

Jesus said, "Everyone who drinks from this water will get thirsty again. But whoever drinks from the water that I will give him will never get thirsty again ever! In fact, the water I will give him will become a well of water springing up within him for eternal life." "Sir," the woman said to Him, "give me this water so I won't get thirsty and come here to draw water." "Go call your husband," He told her, "and come back here." "I don't have a husband," she answered. "You have correctly said, 'I don't have a husband,' " Jesus said. "For you've had five husbands, and the man you now have is not your husband. What you have said is true." "Sir," the woman replied, "I see that You are a prophet. Our fathers worshiped on this mountain, yet you [Jews] say that the place to worship is in Jerusalem."

Man! He knows everything about everybody. — PB

Cool to think we can worship God anywhere. — Tay

Jesus told her, "Believe Me, woman, an hour is coming when you will worship the Father neither on this mountain nor in <u>Jerusalem</u>. You Samaritans worship what you do not know. We worship what we do know, because salvation is from the Jews. But an hour is coming, and is now here, when the true worshipers will worship the Father in spirit and truth. Yes, the Father wants such people to worship Him. God is spirit, and those who worship Him must worship in spirit and truth." The woman said to Him, "I know that Messiah is coming" (who is called Christ). "When He comes, He will explain everything to us." "I am [He]," Jesus told her, "the One speaking to you."

*Big point. Jesus says He is the promised Messiah. That's a huge claim. — Uncle G.

The Ripened Harvest

Just then His disciples arrived, and they were amazed that He was talking with a woman. Yet no one said, "What do You want?" or "Why are You talking with her?"

Then the woman left her water jar, went into town, and told the men, "Come, see a man who told me everything I ever did! Could this be the Messiah?" They left the town and made their way to Him.

Her story was too juicy not to share. I'd tell everyone too! — V

In the meantime the disciples kept urging Him, "Rabbi, eat something." But He said, "I have food to eat that you don't know about." The disciples said to one another, "Could someone have brought Him something to eat?" "My food is to do the will of Him who sent Me and to finish His work," Jesus told them. "Don't you say, 'There are still four more months, then comes the harvest'? Listen [to what] I'm telling you: Open your eyes and look at the fields, for they are ready for harvest. The reaper is already receiving pay and gathering fruit for eternal life, so the sower and reaper can rejoice together. For in this case the saying is true: 'One sows and another reaps.' I sent you to reap what you didn't labor for; others have labored, and you have benefited from their labor."

Good because I'm starving. – PB

He loves to twist things- :)

The Savior of the World

Now many Samaritans from that town believed in Him because of what the woman said when she testified, "He told me everything I ever did." Therefore, when the Samaritans came to Him, they asked Him to stay with them, and He stayed there two days. Many more believed because of what He said. And they told the woman, "We no longer believe because of what you said, for we have heard for ourselves and know that this really is the Savior of the world."

Still freaks me out that he knows everything about everyone. – PB

And my savior too! – Tay

A Galilean Welcome

After two days He left there for Galilee. Jesus Himself testified that a prophet has no honor in his own country. When they entered Galilee, the Galileans welcomed Him because they had seen everything He did in Jerusalem during the festival. For they also had gone to the festival.

These guys party all the time! – PB

The Second Sign: Healing an Official's Son

Then He went again to Cana of Galilee, where He had turned the water into wine. There was a certain royal official whose son was ill at Capernaum. When this man heard that Jesus had come from Judea into Galilee, he went to Him and pleaded with Him to come down and heal his son, for he was about to die. Jesus told him, "Unless you [people] see signs and wonders, you will not believe." "Sir," the official said to Him, "come down before my boy dies!" "Go," Jesus told him, "your son will live."

beats going to the hospital - V

The man believed what Jesus said to him and departed. While he was still going down, his slaves met him saying that his boy was alive. He asked them at what time he got better. "Yesterday at seven in the morning the fever left him," they answered. The father realized this was the very hour at which Jesus had told him, "Your son will live." Then he himself believed, along with his whole household. This therefore was the second sign Jesus performed after He came from Judea to Galilee.

Not sure my dad would believe even if he saw Jesus heal that kid. - Tay

CHAPTER 5

The Third Sign: Healing the Sick

After this, a Jewish festival took place, and Jesus went up to Jerusalem. By the Sheep Gate in Jerusalem there is a pool, called Bethesda in Hebrew, which has five colonnades. Within these lay a multitude of the sick—blind, lame, and paralyzed [—waiting for the moving of the water, because an angel would go down into the pool from time to time and stir up the water. Then the first one who got in after the water was stirred up recovered from whatever ailment he had].

I wonder if an angel still goes down to that pool today. - V

One man was there who had been sick for 38 years. When Jesus saw him lying there and knew he had already been there a long time, He said to him, "Do you want to get well?" "Sir," the sick man answered, "I don't have a man to put me into the pool when the water is stirred up, but while I'm coming, someone goes down ahead of me."

"Get up," Jesus told him, "pick up your bedroll and walk!" Instantly the man got well, picked up his bedroll, and started to walk.

Now that day was the Sabbath, so the Jews said to the man who had been healed, "This is the Sabbath! It's illegal for you to pick up your bedroll." He replied, "The man who made me well told me, 'Pick up your bedroll and walk.'" "Who is this man who told you, 'Pick up [your bedroll] and walk?'" they asked. But the man who was cured did not know who it was, because Jesus had slipped away into the crowd that was there. After this, Jesus found him in the temple complex and said to him, "See, you are well. Do not sin any more, so that something worse doesn't happen to you." The man went and reported to the Jews that it was Jesus who had made him well.

Honoring the Father and the Son

Therefore, the Jews began persecuting Jesus because He was doing these things on the Sabbath. But Jesus responded to them, "My Father is still working, and I am working also." This is why the Jews began trying all the more to kill Him: not only was He breaking the Sabbath, but He was even calling God His own Father, making Himself equal with God.

Then Jesus replied, "I assure you: The Son is not able to do anything on His own, but only what He sees the Father doing. For whatever the Father does, the Son also does these things in the same way. For the Father loves the Son and shows

---

Handwritten margin notes:

Some days I'd much rather stay home sick from school than to get better and have to go. – D

That's the day we're supposed to rest. It's one of the 10 commandments. – Tay

Pretty sure you couldn't slip away today. The news would be all over this stuff. – D

For real – if I saw that happen I think I'd want to follow Jesus around just to see what he was going to do next. – PB

Seems like a stupid rule! – PB

I could see how that would make them nervous. – D

Him everything He is doing, and He will show Him greater works than these so that you will be amazed. And just as the Father raises the dead and gives them life, so the Son also gives life to anyone He wants to. The Father, in fact, judges no one but has given all judgment to the Son, so that all people will honor the Son just as they honor the Father. Anyone who does not honor the Son does not honor the Father who sent Him.

Can't imagine that kind of power. – PB

*Growing up we used to go to my Grandma's house every Sunday afternoon. We'd just sit around doing nothing but talking, except for when it was time for sweets. (Grandma made this amazing apple pie with cinnamon and homemade ice cream on top.) But my momma would always say we needed our Sabbath rest 'cause that's the way God made us.' Keeping the Sabbath day holy is one of the 10 commandments and Jesus talks more about it. In the Bible in the book of Mark, chapter 2 verse 27 Jesus says that the Sabbath was made for man to make sure we got regular rest and a day set apart for God. Seems like the religious leaders in Jesus' time took it a little too far.

– Uncle G.

Life and Judgment

"I assure you: Anyone who hears My word and <u>believes</u> Him who sent Me has eternal life and will not come under judgment but has passed from death to life."

I hear people who say they believe in Jesus live like they don't believe. Seems like believing should change everything. — Tay

"I assure you: An hour is coming, and is now here, when the dead will hear the voice of the Son of God, and those who hear will live. For just as the Father has life in Himself, so also He has granted to the Son to have life in Himself. And He has granted Him the right to pass judgment, because He is the Son of Man. Do not be amazed at this, because a time is coming when all who are in the graves will hear His voice and come out—those who have done good things, to the resurrection of life, but those who have done wicked things, to the resurrection of judgment. "I can do nothing on My own. I judge only as I hear, and My judgment is righteous, because I do not seek My own will, but the will of Him who sent Me."

scary! — √

Four Witnesses to Jesus

"If I testify about Myself, My testimony is not valid. There is Another who testifies about Me, and I know that the testimony He gives about Me is valid."

"You have sent [messengers] to John, and he has testified to the truth. I don't receive man's testimony, but I say these things so that you may be saved."

"John was a burning and shining lamp, and for a time you were willing to enjoy his light. But I have a greater testimony than John's because of the works that the Father has given Me to accomplish. These very works I am doing testify about Me that the Father has sent Me. The Father who sent Me has Himself testified about Me."

"You have not heard His voice at any time, and you haven't seen His form. You don't have His word living in you, because you don't believe the One He sent. You pore over the Scriptures because you think you have eternal life in them, yet they testify about Me. And you are not willing to come to Me that you may have life."

Jesus is like, "Hello. I'm right here. The one you've been waiting for. — Tay

"I do not accept glory from men, but I know you—that you have no love for God within you. I have come in My Father's name, yet you don't accept Me. If someone else comes in his own name, you will accept him. How can you believe? While accepting glory from one another, you don't seek the glory that comes from the only God. Do not think that I will accuse you to the Father. Your accuser is Moses, on whom you have set your hope. For if you believed Moses, you would believe Me, because he wrote about Me. But if you don't believe his writings, how will you believe My words?"

Didn't know Jesus went off on people like that. — V

CHAPTER 6

The Fourth Sign: Feeding 5,000
After this, Jesus crossed the Sea of Galilee (or Tiberias). And a huge crowd was following Him because they saw the signs that He was performing on the sick. So Jesus went up a mountain and sat down there with His disciples. Now the Passover, a Jewish festival, was near.

Sounds much better than going to my boring church. — V

Therefore, when Jesus looked up and noticed a huge crowd coming toward Him, He asked Philip, "Where will we buy bread so these people can eat?" He asked this to test him, for He Himself knew what He was going to do. Philip answered, "Two hundred denarii worth of bread wouldn't be enough for each of them to have a little." One of His disciples, Andrew, Simon Peter's brother, said to Him, "There's a boy here who has five barley loaves and two fish—but what are they for so many?" Then Jesus said, "Have the people sit down." There was plenty of grass in that place, so they sat down. The men numbered about 5,000.

Then Jesus took the loaves, and after giving thanks He distributed them to those who were seated—so also with the fish, as much as they wanted. When they were full, He told His disciples, "Collect the leftovers so that nothing is wasted." So they collected them and filled 12 baskets with the pieces from the five barley loaves that were left over by those who had eaten. When the people saw the sign He had done, they said, "This really is the Prophet who was to come into the world!" Therefore, when Jesus knew that they were about to come and take Him by force to make Him king, He withdrew again to the mountain by Himself.

The Fifth Sign: Walking on Water

When evening came, His disciples went down to the sea, got into a boat, and started across the sea to Capernaum. Darkness had already set in, but Jesus had not yet come to them. Then a high wind arose, and the sea began to churn.

After they had rowed about three or four miles, they saw Jesus walking on the sea. He was coming near the boat, and they were afraid. But He said to them,

Handwritten margin notes:

Hate tests! - V

Not sure I get how this happened. So, did the fish and bread just keep multiplying right in front of the people or what? Wonder what it looked like. - PB

Big lunch for 1 boy. - D

The Jewish people (God's people) thought the Messiah was going to be their king here on earth. Kind of like if we saw someone doing amazing things we might want to make him our president. -Uncle G.

"It is I. Don't be afraid!" Then they were willing to take Him on board, and at once the boat was at the shore where they were heading.

I would've been scared too! Must be cool to walk on water though. – V

The Bread of Life

The next day, the crowd that had stayed on the other side of the sea knew there had been only one boat. [They also knew] that Jesus had not boarded the boat with His disciples, but that His disciples had gone off alone. Some boats from Tiberias came near the place where they ate the bread after the Lord gave thanks.

When the crowd saw that neither Jesus nor His disciples were there, they got into the boats and went to Capernaum looking for Jesus. When they found Him on the other side of the sea, they said to Him, "Rabbi, when did You get here?"

Jesus answered, "I assure you: You are looking for Me, not because you saw the signs, but because you ate the loaves and were filled. Don't work for the food that perishes but for the food that lasts for eternal life, which the Son of Man will give you, because God the Father has set His seal of approval on Him."

You're coming for the FREE FOOD! – PB

How can we get in on this doing miracles thing? Could make some big bucks with that kind of power. – D

"What can we do to perform the works of God?" they asked. Jesus replied, "This is the work of God: that you believe in the One He has sent."

"What sign then are You going to do so we may see and believe You?" they asked. "What are You going to perform? Our fathers ate the manna in the wilderness, just as it is written: He gave them bread from heaven to eat."

I don't get these people. He just made bread and fish appear to feed over 5,000 people and they still don't believe Him? What's up with that? – Tay

Jesus said to them, "I assure you: Moses didn't give you the bread from heaven, but My Father gives you the real bread from heaven. For the bread of God is the One who comes down from heaven and gives life to the world." Then they said, "Sir, give us this bread always!"

Big promises - never hungry or thirsty. But I guess he did just feed a ton of people. - D

"I am the bread of life," Jesus told them. "No one who comes to Me will ever be (hungry) and no one who believes in Me will ever be thirsty again. But as I told you, you've seen Me, and yet you do not believe. Everyone the Father gives Me will come to Me, and the one who comes to Me I will never cast out. For I have come down from heaven, not to do My will, but the will of Him who sent Me. This is the will of Him who sent Me: that I should lose none of those He has given Me but should raise them up on the last day. For this is the will of My Father: that everyone who sees the Son and believes in Him may have eternal life, and I will raise him up on the last day."

God's will in a nutshell. — Tay

Therefore the Jews started complaining about Him, because He said, "I am the bread that came down from heaven." They were saying, "Isn't this Jesus the son of Joseph, whose father and mother we know? How can He now say, 'I have come down from heaven'?" Jesus answered them, "Stop complaining among yourselves. No one can come to Me unless the Father who sent Me draws him, and I will raise him up on the last day.

Tough to escape where you come from. Trust me, I know. - PB

It is written in the Prophets: And they will all be taught by God. Everyone who has listened to and learned from the Father comes to Me— not that anyone has seen the Father except the One who is from God. He has seen the Father. I assure you: Anyone who believes has eternal life. I am the bread of life. Your fathers ate the manna in the wilderness, and they died. This is the bread that comes down from heaven so that anyone may eat of it and not die. I am the living bread that came down from heaven. If anyone eats of this bread he will live forever. The bread that I will give for the life of the world is My flesh."

At that, the Jews argued among themselves, "How can this man give us His flesh to eat?" So Jesus said to them, "I assure you: Unless you eat the flesh of the Son of Man and drink His blood, you do not have life in yourselves. Anyone who eats My flesh and drinks My blood has eternal life, and I will raise him up on the last day, because My flesh is real food and My blood is real drink. The one who eats My flesh and drinks My blood lives in Me, and I in him. Just as the living Father sent Me and I live because of the Father, so the one who feeds on Me will live because of Me. This is the bread that came down from heaven; it is not like the manna your fathers ate—and they died. The one who eats this bread will live forever." He said these things while teaching in the synagogue in Capernaum.

Seems gross. Not sure I get what he's talking about here – V

I don't think he's talking about literally eating his body and blood, but more like a spiritual way of thinking about it — at least that's what my youth leader said. — Tay

Many Disciples Desert Jesus

Therefore, when many of His disciples heard this, they said, "This teaching is hard! Who can accept it?" Jesus, knowing in Himself that His disciples were complaining about this, asked them, "Does this offend you? Then what if you were to observe the Son of Man ascending to where He was before? The Spirit is the One who gives life. The flesh doesn't help at all. The words that I have spoken to you are spirit and are life. But there are some among you who don't believe." (For Jesus knew from the beginning those who would not believe and the one who would betray Him.)

Weird to know someone is going to stab you in the back and you still hang out with them. Don't think I could do that. – D

He said, "This is why I told you that no one can come to Me unless it is granted to him by the Father."

From that moment many of His disciples turned back and no longer accompanied Him. Therefore Jesus said to the Twelve, "You don't want to go away too, do you?" Simon Peter answered, "Lord, who will we go to? You have the words of <u>eternal life</u>. We have come to believe and know that You are the Holy One of God!" Jesus replied to them, "Didn't I choose you, the Twelve? Yet one of you is the Devil!" He was referring to Judas, Simon Iscariot's son, one of the Twelve, because he was going to betray Him.

I love this verse. I try to tell my friends that Jesus is the only one who can give us eternal life. Sometimes they just don't want to listen.
— Tay

CHAPTER 7

The Unbelief of Jesus' Brothers

After this, Jesus traveled in Galilee, since He did not want to travel in Judea because the Jews were trying to kill Him. The Jewish Festival of Tabernacles was near, so His brothers said to Him, "Leave here and go to Judea so Your disciples can see Your works that You are doing. For no one does anything in secret while he's seeking public recognition. If You do these things, show Yourself to the world." (For not even His brothers believed in Him.) *I know what that's like.*
— Tay

Jesus told them, "My time has not yet arrived, but your time is always at hand. The world cannot hate you, but it does hate Me because I testify about it—that its deeds are (evil.) Go up to the festival yourselves. I'm not going up to the festival yet, because My time has not yet fully come." After He had said these things, He stayed in Galilee.

Tells it like it is — which is cool — D

Jesus at the Festival of Tabernacles

After His brothers had gone up to the festival, then He also went up, not openly but secretly. The Jews were looking for Him at the festival and saying, "Where is He?" And there was a lot of discussion about Him among the crowds. Some were saying, "He's a good man." Others were saying, "No, on the contrary, He's deceiving the people." Still, nobody was talking publicly about Him because they feared the Jews.

When the festival was already half over, Jesus went up into the temple complex and began to teach. Then the Jews were amazed and said, "How does He know the Scriptures, since He hasn't been trained?" Jesus answered them, "My teaching isn't Mine but is from the One who sent Me. If anyone wants to do His will, he will understand whether the teaching is from God or if I am speaking on My own. The one who speaks for himself seeks his own glory. But He who seeks the glory of the One who sent Him is true, and there is no unrighteousness in Him. Didn't Moses give you the law? Yet none of you keeps the law! Why do you want to kill Me?"

"You have a demon!" the crowd responded.
"Who wants to kill You?"

"I did one work, and you are all amazed," Jesus answered. "Consider this: Moses has given you circumcision—not that it comes from Moses but from the fathers—and you circumcise a man on the Sabbath. If a man receives circumcision on the Sabbath so that the law of Moses won't be broken, are you angry at Me because I made a man entirely well on the Sabbath? Stop judging according to outward appearances; rather judge according to righteous judgment."

The Identity of the Messiah

Some of the people of Jerusalem were saying, "Isn't this the man they want to kill? Yet, look! He's speaking publicly and they're saying nothing to Him. Can it be true that the authorities know He is the Messiah? But we know where this man is from. When the (Messiah) comes, nobody will know where He is from."

Did they know he really was the Messiah? - D

As He was teaching in the temple complex, Jesus cried out, "You know Me and you know where I am from. Yet I have not come on My own, but the One who sent Me is true. You don't know Him; I know Him because I am from Him, and He sent Me."

Now that is sweet - D

Then they tried to seize Him. Yet no one laid a hand on Him because His hour had not yet (come.) However, many from the crowd believed in Him and said, "When the Messiah comes, He won't perform more signs than this man has done, will He?" The Pharisees heard the crowd muttering these things about Him, so the chief priests and the Pharisees sent temple police to arrest Him.

On what charge? Doesn't seem right. - PB

Then Jesus said, "I am only with you for a short time. Then I'm going to the One who sent Me. You will look for Me, but you will not find Me; and where I am, you cannot come."

Then the Jews said to one another, "Where does He intend to go so we won't find Him? He doesn't intend to go to the Dispersion among the Greeks and teach the Greeks, does He? What is this remark He made: 'You will <u>look</u> for Me, and you will not find Me; and where I am, you cannot come'?"

Ultimate hide and go seek. — Tay

The Promise of the Spirit

On the last and most important day of the festival, Jesus stood up and cried out, "If anyone is thirsty, he should come to Me and drink! The one who believes in Me, as the Scripture has said, will have streams of living water flow from deep within him." He said this about the Spirit, whom those who believed in Him were going to <u>receive</u>, for the Spirit had not yet been received, because Jesus had not yet been glorified. *I was taught that when I believed in Jesus as my Savior, the Holy Spirit came to live inside of me. — Tay*

The People Are Divided over Jesus

When some from the crowd heard these words, they said, "This really is the Prophet!" Others said, "This is the Messiah!" But some said, "Surely the Messiah doesn't come from Galilee, does He? Doesn't the Scripture say that the Messiah comes from David's offspring and from the town of Bethlehem, where David once lived?" So a division occurred among the crowd because of Him. Some of them wanted to seize Him, but no one laid hands on Him. *So much for peace and unity. Jesus seems to divide everyone more than bring them together. — V*

Debate over Jesus' Claims

Then the temple police came to the chief priests and Pharisees, who asked them, "Why haven't you brought Him?" The police answered, "No man ever spoke like (this!)" Then the Pharisees responded to them: "Are you fooled too? Have any of the rulers believed in Him? Or any of the Pharisees? But this crowd, which doesn't know the law, is accursed!"

Funny ... the cops don't want to arrest him. — D

Nicodemus—the one who came to Him previously, being one of them—said to them, "Our law doesn't judge a man before it hears from him and knows what he's doing, does it?" "You aren't from Galilee too, are you?" they replied.

"Investigate and you will see that no prophet arises from Galilee." [So each one went to his house.]

Jesus seems to have these religious leaders freaking out a bit. – V

CHAPTER 8

But Jesus went to the Mount of Olives.

Yummy! Love olives! Hmmm that's kind of cheesy I guess – V

An Adulteress Forgiven

At dawn He went to the temple complex again, and all the people were coming to Him. He sat down and began to teach them. Then the scribes and the Pharisees brought a woman caught in adultery, making her stand in the center. "Teacher," they said to Him, "this woman was caught in the act of committing adultery. In the law Moses commanded us to stone such women. So what do You say?" They asked this to trap Him, in order that they might have evidence to accuse Him.

Don't mess with the Son of God. – Tay

Wonder what he was writing. It sure chased them off. Maybe he was listing their sins or something like that I would take off too if he started listing mine for everyone to see. – D

Jesus stooped down and started writing on the ground with His finger. When they persisted in questioning Him, He stood up and said to them, "The one without sin among you should be the first to throw a stone at her." Then He stooped down again and continued writing on the ground. When they heard this, they left one by one, starting with the older men.

Only He was left, with the woman in the center. When Jesus stood up, He said to her, "Woman, where are they? Has no one condemned you?" "No one, Lord," she answered. "Neither do I condemn you," said Jesus. "Go, and from now on do not sin any more."

Wow, she went from almost being stoned to death, to a new start. I'd love a new start like that. – V

The Light of the World

Then Jesus spoke to them again: "I am the light of the world. Anyone who follows Me will never walk in the darkness but will have the light of life." So the Pharisees said to Him, "You are testifying about Yourself. Your testimony is not valid."

"Even if I testify about Myself," Jesus replied, "My testimony is valid, because I know where I came from and where I'm going. But you don't know where I come from or where I'm going. You judge by human standards. I judge no one. And if I do judge, My judgment is true, because I am not alone, but I and the Father who sent Me [judge together]. Even in your law it is written that the witness of two men is valid. I am the One who testifies about Myself, and the Father who sent Me testifies about Me.

Tricky. – D

Then they asked Him, "Where is Your Father?" "You know neither Me nor My Father," Jesus answered. "If you knew Me, you would also know My Father." He spoke these words by the treasury, while teaching in the temple complex. But no one seized Him, because His hour had not come.

It keeps saying this... very cool every time. Can't touch me yet! – PB

Jesus Predicts His Departure

Then He said to them again, "I'm going away; you will look for Me, and you will die in your sin. Where I'm going, you cannot come." So the Jews said again, "He won't kill Himself, will He, since He says, 'Where I'm going, you cannot come'?" "You are from below," **He told them,** "I am from above. You are of this world; I am not of this world. Therefore I told you that you will die in your sins. For if you do not believe that I am [He], you will die in your sins."

Sounds like he's saying he's an alien - D

It's all about believing again I'm getting the point. - V

"Who are You?" they questioned. "Precisely what I've been telling you from the very beginning," **Jesus told them,** "I have many things to say and to judge about you, but the One who sent Me is true, and what I have heard from Him—these things I tell the world."

Nobody seems to get him. I know the feeling. - V

They did not know He was speaking to them about the Father. So Jesus said to them, "When you lift up the Son of Man, then you will know that I am [He], and that I do nothing on My own. But just as the Father taught Me, I say these things. The One who sent Me is with Me. He has not left Me alone, because I always do what pleases Him."

Wish I could say the same. - Tay

Heard this before but didn't know it was Jesus who said it. Seems like he's saying his Word is the truth and that's what sets you free. Different than how I heard it before - D

Truth and Freedom

As He was saying these things, many believed in Him. So Jesus said to the Jews who had believed Him, "If you continue in My word, you really are My disciples. You will know the truth, and the truth will set you free." "We are descendants of Abraham," they answered Him, "and we have never been enslaved to anyone. "How can You say, 'You will become free'?" **Jesus responded,** "I assure you: Everyone who commits sin is a slave of sin. A slave does not remain in the household forever, but a son does remain forever. Therefore if the Son sets you free, you really will be free. I know you are descendants of Abraham, but you are trying to kill Me because My word is not welcome among you. I speak what I have seen in the presence of the Father, and therefore you do what you have heard from your father." *From slave to son - very cool. - V*

"Our father is Abraham!" they replied. "If you were Abraham's children," Jesus told them, "you would do what Abraham did. But now you are trying to kill Me, a man who has told you the truth that I heard from God. Abraham did not do this! You're doing what your father does."

→ Not pulling any punches. - PB

"We weren't born of sexual immorality," they said. "We have one Father— God." Jesus said to them, "If God were your Father, you would love Me, because I came from God and I am here. For I didn't come on My own, but He sent Me. Why don't you understand what I say? Because you cannot listen to My word. You are of your father the Devil, and you want to carry out your father's desires. He was a murderer from the beginning and has not stood in the truth, because there is no truth in him. When he tells a lie, he speaks from his own nature, because he is a liar and the father of liars. Yet because I tell the truth, you do not believe Me. Who among you can convict Me of sin?

Left hook to the jaw! - PB

Massive uppercut! - PB

If I tell the truth, why don't you believe Me? The one who is from God listens to God's words. This is why you don't listen, because you are not from God."

Knockout! - PB

Jesus and Abraham

The Jews responded to Him, "Aren't we right in saying that You're a Samaritan and have a demon?"

Hey man don't you have a demon? Crazy - D

"I do not have a demon," Jesus answered. "On the contrary, I honor My Father and you dishonor Me. I do not seek My glory; the One who seeks it also judges. I assure you: If anyone keeps My word, he will never see death—ever!"

Then the Jews said, "Now we know You have a demon. Abraham died and so did the prophets. You say, 'If anyone keeps My word, he will never taste death—ever!' Are You greater than our father Abraham who died? Even the prophets died. Who do You pretend to be?" *Calling him a poser. - PB*

"If I glorify Myself," Jesus answered, "My glory is nothing. My Father—you say about Him, 'He is our God'—He is the One who glorifies Me. You've never known Him, but I know Him. If I were to say I don't know Him, I would be a liar like you. But I do know Him, and I keep His word. Your father Abraham was overjoyed that he would see My day; he saw it and rejoiced." *Back at it again! - PB*

The Jews replied, "You aren't 50 years old yet, and You've seen Abraham?" Jesus said to them, "I assure you: Before Abraham was, I am." At that, they picked up stones to throw at Him. But Jesus was hidden and went out of the temple complex.

My pastor said it's a big deal when Jesus says "I am" because that's how God talked about Himself in the Old Testament part of the Bible. For Jesus to claim to be the "I am" was like total blasphemy to the Jewish leaders. That's probably why they grabbed rocks to throw at him.
— Tay

CHAPTER 9

The Sixth Sign: Healing a Man Born Blind

As He was passing by, He saw a man blind from birth. His disciples questioned Him: " Rabbi, who sinned, this man or his parents, that he was born blind?" "Neither this man nor his parents sinned," Jesus answered. "[This came about] so that God's works might be displayed in him. We must do the works of Him who sent Me while it is day. Night is coming when no one can work. As long as I am in the world, I am the light of the world."

A purpose for blindness? My sister is deaf, wonder what the purpose is for that? - PB

After He said these things He spit on the ground, made some mud from the saliva, and spread the mud on his eyes "Go," He told him, "wash in the pool of Siloam" (which means "Sent"). So he left, washed, and came back seeing.

Nasty! – V

Wonder why he used mud this time? – D

His neighbors and those who formerly had seen him as a beggar said, "Isn't this the man who sat begging?" Some said, "He's the one." "No," others were saying, "but he looks like him." He kept saying, "I'm the one!" Therefore they asked him, "Then how were your eyes opened?" He answered, "The man called Jesus made mud, spread it on my eyes, and told me, 'Go to Siloam and wash.' So when I went and washed I received my sight." "Where is He?" they asked. "I don't know," he said.

can't imagine trying to get people to believe you – V

The Healed Man's Testimony

They brought the man who used to be blind to the Pharisees. The day that Jesus made the mud and opened his eyes was a Sabbath. So again the Pharisees asked him how he received his sight. "He put mud on my eyes," he told them. "I washed and I can see." Therefore some of the Pharisees said, "This man is not from God, for He doesn't keep the Sabbath!" But others were saying, "How can a sinful man perform such signs?" And there was a division among them.

Shaking things up again – my kind of guy. – PB

I don't get these Pharisee people. He does something good again on the Sabbath and they don't like it – D

Again they asked the blind man, "What do you say about Him, since He opened your eyes?" "He's a prophet," he said. The Jews did not believe this about him—that he was blind and received sight—until they summoned the parents of the one who had received his sight. They asked them, "Is this your son, [the one] you say was born blind? How then does he now see?"

"We know this is our son and that he was born blind," his parents answered. "But we don't know how he now sees, and we don't know who opened his eyes. Ask him; he's of age. He will speak for himself." His parents said these things because they were afraid of the Jews since the Jews had already agreed that if anyone confessed Him as Messiah, he would be banned from the synagogue. This is why his parents said, "He's of age; ask him."

So a second time they summoned the man who had been blind and told him, "Give glory to God. We know that this man is a sinner!" He answered, "Whether or not He's a sinner, I don't know. One thing I do know: I was blind, and now I can see!"

Then they asked him, "What did He do to you? How did He open your eyes?" "I already told you," he said, "and you didn't listen. Why do you want to hear it again? You don't want to become His disciples too, do you?"

They ridiculed him: "You're that man's disciple, but we're Moses' disciples. We know that God has spoken to Moses. But this man—we don't know where He's from!" "This is an amazing thing," the man told them. "You don't know where He is from, yet He opened my eyes! We know that God doesn't listen to sinners, but if anyone is God-fearing and does His will, He listens to him. Throughout history no one has ever heard of someone opening the eyes of a person born blind. If this man were not from God, He wouldn't be able to do anything." "You were born entirely in sin," they replied, "and are you trying to teach us?" Then they threw him out.

The Blind Man's Sight and the Pharisees' Blindness

When Jesus heard that they had thrown the man out, He found him and asked,
"Do you believe in the Son of Man?" "Who is He, Sir, that I may believe in Him?"
he asked. Jesus answered, "You have seen Him; in fact, He is the One speaking
with you." "I believe, Lord!" he said, and he worshiped Him.

> → Tough to not believe when you were blind and now you're not. – PB

Jesus said, "I came into this world for judgment, in order that those who do not
see will see and those who do see will become blind." Some of the Pharisees who
were with Him heard these things and asked Him, "We aren't blind too, are we?"
"If you were blind," Jesus told them, "you wouldn't have sin. But now that you
say, 'We see'—your sin remains."

> Sometimes he says confusing things that I have to really think about. – V

CHAPTER 10

> Dad took me to a petting zoo once. I learned that sheep's wool feels strange and its not a good idea to try to head butt a goat. – D

The Ideal Shepherd

"I assure you: Anyone who doesn't enter the sheep pen by the door but climbs
in some other way, is a thief and a robber. The one who enters by the door is
the shepherd of the sheep. The doorkeeper opens it for him, and the sheep
hear his voice. He calls his own sheep by name and leads them out. When
he has brought all his own outside, he goes ahead of them. The sheep follow
him because they recognize his voice. They will never follow a stranger;
instead they will run away from him, because they don't recognize the voice of
strangers." Jesus gave them this illustration, but they did not understand what
He was telling them.

> Me either. – V

The Good Shepherd

So Jesus said again, "I assure you: I am the door of the sheep. All who came before Me are thieves and robbers, but the sheep didn't listen to them. I am the door. If anyone enters by Me, he will be saved and will come in and go out and find pasture. A thief comes only to steal and to kill and to destroy. I have come that they may have life and have it in <u>abundance.</u> I am the good shepherd. The good shepherd lays down his life for the sheep. The hired man, since he is not the shepherd and doesn't own the sheep, leaves them and runs away when he sees a wolf coming. The wolf then snatches and scatters them. [This happens because he is a hired man and doesn't care about the sheep.]

Ah.. foreshadowing. English class taught me something. — PB

I am the good shepherd. I know My own sheep, and they know Me, as the Father knows Me, and I know the Father. I lay down My life for the sheep. But I have other sheep that are not of this fold; I must bring them also, and they will listen to My voice. Then there will be one flock, one shepherd.

I hope I'm one of them. — V

This is why the Father loves Me, because I am laying down My life so I may take it up again. No one takes it from Me, but I lay it down on My own. I have the right to lay it down, and I have the right to take it up again. I have received this command from My Father."

I think a lot of people believe that if they decided to follow Jesus that life would be lame and boring. I like this part because Jesus is saying that the best life comes when you follow him. — Tay

Guess he's saying that he could've avoided being killed, but he allowed himself to be killed for the sake of his sheep. That changes things for me. I thought they just took him and killed him. — D

Again a division took place among the Jews because of these words. Many of them were saying, "He has a demon and He's crazy! Why do you listen to Him?" Others were saying, "These aren't the words of someone demon-possessed. Can a demon open the eyes of the blind?"

⤷ Split decision. — PB

Jesus at the Festival of Dedication

[handwritten: Wonder if they get snow? - V ♡]

Then the Festival of Dedication took place in Jerusalem, and it was winter. Jesus was walking in the temple complex in Solomon's Colonnade. Then the Jews surrounded Him and asked, "How long are You going to keep us in suspense? If You are the Messiah, tell us plainly."

"I did tell you and you don't believe," Jesus answered them. "The works that I do in My Father's name testify about Me. But you don't believe because you are not My sheep. My sheep hear My voice, I know them, and they follow Me. I give them eternal life, and they will never perish—ever! No one will snatch them out of My hand. My Father, who has given them to Me, is greater than all. No one is able to snatch them out of the Father's hand. The Father and I are one.*"

*[handwritten: *He's saying He is one with God -that He is divine. That really seems to upset the Jews as being blasphemous. -Uncle G.]*

Renewed Efforts to Stone Jesus

Again the Jews picked up rocks to stone Him. Jesus replied, "I have shown you many good works from the Father. Which of these works are you stoning Me for?"

[handwritten: →Good question. - PB]

"We aren't stoning You for a good work," the Jews answered, "but for blasphemy, because You—being a man—make Yourself God." Jesus answered them, "Isn't it written in your law, I said, you are gods? If He called those whom the word of God came to 'gods'—and the Scripture cannot be broken— do you say, 'You are blaspheming' to the One the Father set apart and sent into the world, because I said: I am the Son of God? If I am not doing My Father's works, don't believe Me. But if I am doing them and you don't believe Me, believe the works. This way you will know and understand that the Father is in Me and I in the Father." Then they were trying again to seize Him, yet He eluded their grasp.

Take your pick. - D

He has great escapability. - PB

Many beyond the Jordan Believe in Jesus

So He departed again across the Jordan to the place where John had been baptizing earlier, and He remained there. Many came to Him and said, "John never did a sign, but everything John said about this man was true." And many believed in Him there.

CHAPTER 11

Lazarus Dies at Bethany

Now a man was sick, Lazarus, from Bethany, the village of Mary and her sister Martha. Mary was the one who anointed the Lord with fragrant oil and wiped His feet with her hair, and it was her brother Lazarus who was sick. So the sisters sent a message to Him: "Lord, the one You love is sick."

That's kind of gross! - V

When Jesus heard it, He said, "This sickness will not end in death but is for the glory of God, so that the Son of God may be glorified through it." (Jesus loved Martha, her sister, and Lazarus.) So when He heard that he was sick, He stayed two more days in the place where He was. Then after that, He said to the disciples, "Let's go to Judea again."

"Rabbi," the disciples told Him, "just now the Jews tried to stone You, and You're going there again?"

They must think he's crazy. - D

"Aren't there 12 hours in a day?" **Jesus answered.** "If anyone walks during the day, he doesn't stumble, because he sees the light of this world. If anyone walks during the night, he does stumble, because the light is not in him."

Not sure what that has to do with getting stoned by the Jews???? - PB

He said this, and then He told them, "Our friend Lazarus has fallen asleep, but I'm on My way to wake him up." **Then the disciples said to Him,** "Lord, if he has fallen asleep, he will get well." **Jesus, however, was speaking about his death, but they thought He was speaking about natural sleep.**

Seems like you need a secret decoder ring sometimes to figure out what Jesus is saying, or maybe I'm just a geek. - D

So Jesus then told them plainly, "Lazarus has died. I'm glad for you that I wasn't there so that you may believe. But let's go to him." **Then Thomas (called "Twin") said to his fellow disciples,** "Let's go so that we may die with Him."

Uh, yeah, I'll be right behind you - D

The Resurrection and the Life

When Jesus arrived, He found that Lazarus had already been in the tomb four days. Bethany was near Jerusalem (about two miles away). Many of the Jews had come to Martha and Mary to comfort them about their brother. As soon as Martha heard that Jesus was coming, she went to meet Him. But Mary remained seated in the house. Then Martha said to Jesus, "Lord, if You had been here, my brother wouldn't have died. Yet even now I know that whatever You ask from God, God will give You."

"Your brother will rise again," **Jesus told her.** Martha said, "I know that he will rise again in the resurrection at the last day." **Jesus said to her,** "I am the resurrection and the life. The one who believes in Me, even if he dies, will live. Everyone who lives and believes in Me will never die—ever. Do you believe this?"

Heard this at Easter. - V

Believe, believe, believe. Wonder how many times Jesus says "Believe"? - PB

"Yes, Lord," she told Him, "I believe You are the Messiah, the Son of God, who was to come into the world."

Jesus Shares the Sorrow of Death

Having said this, she went back and called her sister Mary, saying in private, "The Teacher is here and is calling for you." As soon as she heard this, she got up quickly and went to Him. Jesus had not yet come into the village but was still in the place where Martha had met Him.

The Jews who were with her in the house consoling her saw that Mary got up quickly and went out. So they followed her, supposing that she was going to the tomb to cry there. When Mary came to where Jesus was and saw Him, she fell at His feet and told Him, "Lord, if You had been here, my brother would not have died!" *She had some real faith.* — Tay

When Jesus saw her crying, and the Jews who had come with her crying, He was angry in His spirit and deeply moved. "Where have you put him?" He asked. "Lord," they told Him, "come and see." Jesus wept. So the Jews said, "See how He loved him!" But some of them said, "Couldn't He who opened the blind man's eyes also have kept this man from dying?" *Jesus cries? This is probably the coolest part for me so far. Nice to know that even though He's perfect and divine that he still cries when he sees people he loves crying.* — V

The Seventh Sign: Raising Lazarus from the Dead

crying and angry? Wow. — V

Then Jesus, angry in Himself again, came to the tomb. It was a cave, and a stone was lying against it. "Remove the stone," Jesus said. Martha, the dead man's sister, told Him, "Lord, he already stinks. It's been four days."

New cologne – Ode to Dead Body. Nasty. — PB

Jesus said to her, "Didn't I tell you that if you believed you would see the glory of God?" So they removed the stone.

Then Jesus raised His eyes and said, "Father, I thank You that You heard Me. I know that You always hear Me, but because of the crowd standing here I said this, so they may believe You sent Me." After He said this, He shouted with a loud voice, "Lazarus, come out!" The dead man came out bound hand and foot with linen strips and with his face wrapped in a cloth. Jesus said to them, "Loose him and let him go."

How is this even possible? The guy was dead for four days! Seriously, if I saw this happen, that would be proof enough for me that he was who he said he was. - D

The Plot to Kill Jesus

Therefore many of the Jews who came to Mary and saw what He did believed in Him. But some of them went to the Pharisees and told them what Jesus had done. So the chief priests and the Pharisees convened the Sanhedrin and said, "What are we going to do since this man does many signs? If we let Him continue in this way, everybody will believe in Him! Then the Romans will come and remove both our place and our nation."

This is hilarious! "Oh no, he's doing too much good stuff and everyone will like him! We have to take him out now!" Are you kidding me? - PB

One of them, Caiaphas, who was high priest that year, said to them, "You know nothing at all! You're not considering that it is to your advantage that one man should die for the people rather than the whole nation perish." He did not say this on his own, but being high priest that year he prophesied that Jesus was going to die for the nation, and not for the nation only, but also to unite the scattered children of God. So from that day on they plotted to kill Him.

He got that prophecy right! - Tay

Religious leaders become Hit Men. I used to think Jesus was a nice guy who brought peace and love. Looks more like people either loved him or hated him. - D

Therefore Jesus no longer walked openly among the Jews but departed from there to the countryside near the wilderness, to a town called Ephraim. And He stayed there with the disciples. The Jewish Passover was near, and many went up to Jerusalem from the country to purify themselves before the Passover. They were looking for Jesus and asking one another as they stood in the temple complex: "What do you think? He won't come to the festival, will He?" The chief priests and the Pharisees had given orders that if anyone knew where He was, he should report it so they could arrest Him.

CHAPTER 12

The Anointing at Bethany

Six days before the Passover, Jesus came to Bethany where Lazarus was, the one Jesus had raised from the dead. So they gave a dinner for Him there; Martha was serving them, and Lazarus was one of those reclining at the table with Him. Then Mary took a pound of fragrant oil—pure and expensive nard—anointed Jesus' feet, and wiped His feet with her hair. So the house was filled with the fragrance of the oil. Then one of His disciples, Judas Iscariot (who was about to betray Him), said, "Why wasn't this fragrant oil sold for 300 denarii and given to the poor?" He didn't say this because he cared about the poor but because he was a thief. He was in charge of the money-bag and would steal part of what was put in it. Jesus answered, "Leave her alone; she has kept it for the day of My burial. For you always have the poor with you, but you do not always have Me."

Has his mind on the money and the money on his mind. - PB

It must be weird to know: 1. You're going to be killed even though you're innocent of any crime 2. It's going to hurt big time 3. The people you're dying for are the ones who want to kill you - PB

The Decision to Kill Lazarus

Then a large crowd of the Jews learned He was there. They came not only because of Jesus, but also to see Lazarus the one He had raised from the dead.

Therefore the chief priests decided to also kill Lazarus, because he was the reason many of the Jews were deserting them and believing in Jesus.

Seriously wicked priests! - D

The Triumphal Entry

The next day, when the large crowd that had come to the festival heard that Jesus was coming to Jerusalem, they took palm branches and went out to meet Him. They kept shouting: "Hosanna! Blessed is He who comes in the name of the Lord —the King of Israel!" Jesus found a young donkey and sat on it, just as it is written: Fear no more, Daughter Zion; look! your King is coming, sitting on a donkey's colt.

So much for flying under the radar when people are looking to kill you. - PB

His disciples did not understand these things at first. However, when Jesus was glorified, then they remembered that these things had been written about Him and that they had done these things to Him. Meanwhile the crowd, which had been with Him when He called Lazarus out of the tomb and raised him from the dead, continued to testify. This is also why the crowd met Him, because they heard He had done this sign. Then the Pharisees said to one another, "You see? You've accomplished nothing. Look—the world has gone after Him!"

Jealous? - V

Jesus Predicts His Crucifixion

Now some Greeks were among those who went up to worship at the festival. So they came to Philip, who was from Bethsaida in Galilee, and requested of him, "Sir, we want to see Jesus." Philip went and told Andrew; then Andrew and Philip went and told Jesus.

Jesus replied to them, "The hour has come for the Son of Man to be glorified. I assure you: Unless a grain of wheat falls into the ground and dies, it remains by itself. But if it dies, it produces a large crop. The one who loves his life will lose it, and the one who hates his life in this world will keep it for eternal (life.)

Hmmm. Have to think about that one. - D

If anyone serves Me, he must follow Me. Where I am, there My servant also will be. If anyone serves Me, the Father will honor him. Now My soul is troubled. What should I say—Father, save Me from this hour? But that is why I came to this hour. Father, glorify Your name!"

♡ WOW! - V

Then a voice came from heaven: "I have glorified it, and I will glorify it again!" The crowd standing there heard it and said it was thunder. Others said, "An angel has spoken to Him!"

It would work on me. - V
♡

Jesus responded, "This voice came, not for Me, but for you. Now is the judgment of this world. Now the ruler of this world will be cast out. As for Me, if I am lifted up from the earth I will draw all [people] to Myself."

He said this to signify what kind of death He was about to die. Then the crowd replied to Him, "We have heard from the law that the Messiah will remain forever. So how can You say, 'The Son of Man must be lifted up'? Who is this Son of Man?"

Jesus answered, "The light will be with you only a little longer. Walk while you have the light so that darkness doesn't overtake you. The one who walks in darkness doesn't know where he's going. While you have the light, believe in

the light so that you may become sons of light." Jesus said this, then went away
and hid from them. *He never seems to directly answer any questions. I actually kind of like that about him. He does his own thing. - PB*

Isaiah's Prophecies Fulfilled
Even though He had performed so many signs in their presence, they did not
believe in Him. But this was to fulfill the word of Isaiah the prophet, who said:
"Lord, who has believed our message? And who has the arm of the Lord been
revealed to?" This is why they were unable to believe, because Isaiah also
said: "He has blinded their eyes and hardened their hearts, so that they would
not see with their eyes or understand with their hearts, and be converted, and
I would heal them. Isaiah said these things because he saw His glory and spoke
about Him.

How could they not believe in him after seeing everything he'd done? - V

It's hard to think about God blinding their eyes and hardening their hearts. I wish he'd soften my dad's heart. - Tay

Nevertheless, many did believe in Him even among the rulers, but because of
the Pharisees they did not confess Him, so they would not be banned from the
synagogue. For they loved praise from men more than praise from God.

Can you be a secret believer in Jesus? - Tay

That's me too. But I guess I'm just starting to understand what Jesus and God is all about as I go through this. So maybe things will change. - V

A Summary of Jesus' Mission
Then Jesus cried out, "The one who believes in Me believes not in Me, but in Him
who sent Me. And the one who sees Me sees Him who sent Me. I have come as a
light into the world, so that everyone who believes in Me would not remain in
darkness.

If anyone hears My words and doesn't keep them, I do not judge him; for I did
not come to judge the world but to save the world. The one who rejects Me and
doesn't accept My sayings has this as his judge: the word I have spoken will

judge him on the (last day.) For I have not spoken on My own, but the Father Himself who sent Me has given Me a command as to what I should say and what I should speak. I know that His command is eternal life. So the things that I should speak, I speak just as the Father has told Me."

Must be talking about the judgment day thing. I've heard about that.
— D

CHAPTER 13

→ *You reject me? Deal with my dad!*
— PB

Jesus Washes His Disciples' Feet

Before the Passover Festival, Jesus knew that His hour had come to depart from this world to the Father. Having loved His own who were in the world, He loved them to the end. Now by the time of supper, the Devil had already put it into the heart of Judas, Simon Iscariot's son, to betray Him.

Freaky to think the devil puts stuff in our hearts. — V

Jesus knew that the Father had given everything into His hands, that He had come from God, and that He was going back to God. So He got up from supper, laid aside His robe, took a towel, and tied it around Himself. Next, He poured water into a basin and began to wash His disciples' feet and to dry them with the towel tied around Him.

Feet are nasty! — Tay

He came to Simon Peter, who asked Him, "Lord, are You going to wash my feet?" Jesus answered him, "What I'm doing you don't understand now, but afterwards you will know." "You will never wash my feet—ever!" Peter said. Jesus replied, "If I don't wash you, you have no part with Me."

What's with the foot washing thing? Seems like a weird thing to do.
— D

* When my momma was near the end, I had to do everything for her. Give her baths, cook her food, change her diapers, brush her hair and teeth...everything. It was the most humbling experience of my life. I learned a lot about being a servant. She did all that for me when I was a baby. I think washing feet is like that. Feet back then were nasty because it was dirty and dusty. They probably smelled terrible and were caked with dirt and grime. For the son of God to wash his follower's feet would have been upside down. This shows Jesus being willing to not only die for us, but to stoop to the lowest level to serve us. Amazing!

    - Uncle G.

Simon Peter said to Him, "Lord, not only my feet, but also my hands and my head." "One who has bathed," Jesus told him, "doesn't need to wash anything except his feet, but he is completely clean. You are clean, but not all of you." For He knew who would betray Him. This is why He said, "You are not all clean."

All or nothing. Lord, wash all of me. — Tay

The Meaning of Footwashing

When Jesus had washed their feet and put on His robe, He reclined again and said to them, "Do you know what I have done for you? You call Me Teacher and Lord. This is well said, for I am. So if I, your Lord and Teacher, have washed your feet, you also ought to wash one another's feet. For I have given you an example that you also should do just as I have done for you."

Do Christians do this anymore? — D

"I assure you: A slave is not greater than his master, and a messenger is not greater than the one who sent him. If you know these things, you are blessed if you do them. I'm not speaking about all of you; I know those I have chosen. But the Scripture must be fulfilled: The one who eats My bread has raised his heel against Me." → *Wonder if he winked at Judas when he said this. — PB*

"I am telling you now before it happens, so that when it does happen you will believe that I am [He]. I assure you: The one who receives whomever I send receives Me, and the one who receives Me receives Him who sent Me."

Judas' Betrayal Predicted   *♡ No doubt. — V*

When Jesus had said this, He was troubled in His spirit and testified, "I assure you: One of you will betray Me!"

The disciples started looking at one another—uncertain which one He was speaking about. One of His disciples, the one Jesus loved, was reclining close beside Jesus. Simon Peter motioned to him to find out who it was He was talking about. So he leaned back against Jesus and asked Him, "Lord, who is it?"

I think this Peter guy wanted to crush the traitor before he did the deed. - D

Jesus replied, "He's the one I give the piece of bread to after I have dipped it." When He had dipped the bread, He gave it to Judas, Simon Iscariot's son. After [Judas ate] the piece of bread, Satan entered him.

I don't want to know what that feels like. I wonder if you could tell just by looking at him. Scary. - V

Therefore Jesus told him, "What you're doing, do quickly." None of those reclining at the table knew why He told him this. Since Judas kept the money-bag, some thought that Jesus was telling him, "Buy what we need for the festival," or that he should give something to the poor. After receiving the piece of bread, he went out immediately. And it was night.

Surprised Peter didn't jump across the table and pound him right away. - PB

The New Commandment
When he had gone out, Jesus said, "Now the Son of Man is glorified, and God is glorified in Him. If God is glorified in Him, God will also glorify Him in Himself and will glorify Him at once. Children, I am with you a little while longer. You will look for Me, and just as I told the Jews, 'Where I am going you cannot come,' so now I tell you."

"I give you a new commandment: love one another. Just as I have loved you, you must also love one another. By this all people will know that you are My disciples if you have love for one another."

I've seen a lot of people who call themselves Christians that don't seem to love anybody but themselves. - D

Peter's Denials Predicted

"Lord," Simon Peter said to Him, "where are You going?" Jesus answered, "Where I am going you cannot follow Me now, but you will follow later." "Lord," Peter asked, "why can't I follow You now? I will lay down <u>my life for You</u>!" Jesus replied, "Will you lay down your life for Me? I assure you: A rooster will not crow until you have denied Me three times."

I hope I would've said the same thing. — Tay

CHAPTER 14

The Way to the Father

"Your heart must not be troubled. Believe in God; believe also in Me. In My Father's house are many dwelling places; if not, I would have told you. I am going away to prepare a <u>place for you</u>. If I go away and prepare a place for you, I will come back and receive you to Myself, so that where I am you may be also. You know the way where I am going." *I can't wait until I see the place he prepared for me! — Tay*

"Lord," Thomas said, "we don't know where You're going. How can we know the way?" Jesus told him, "I am the way, the truth, and the life. No one comes to the Father (except through Me.) *Heard this one before. Guess if he says he's the truth then anything that doesn't agree with him is false, right? Big claim, but if he is who he says he is I guess he can say he's the truth - D*

Jesus Reveals the Father

"If you know Me, you will also know My Father. From now on you do know Him and have seen Him." "Lord," said Philip, "show us the Father, and that's enough for us."

Jesus said to him, "Have I been among you all this time without your knowing Me, Philip? The one who has seen Me has seen the Father. How can you say, 'Show us the Father'? Don't you believe that I am in the Father and the Father is in Me? The words I speak to you I do not speak on My own. The Father who lives in Me does His works. Believe Me that I am in the Father and the Father is in Me. Otherwise, believe because of the works themselves."

See my note on the next page.

Kind of weird the whole idea of them being united. – V

Praying in Jesus' Name

"I assure you: The one who believes in Me will also do the works that I do. And he will do even greater works than these, because I am going to the Father. Whatever you ask in My name, I will do it so that the Father may be glorified in the Son. If you ask Me anything in My name, I will do it."

Whoa! Never heard that one. – PB

I think he's talking about doing things for us that honor God. – Tay

Another Counselor Promised

"If you love Me, you will keep My commandments. And I will ask the Father, and He will give you another Counselor to be with you forever. He is the Spirit of truth. The world is unable to receive Him because it doesn't see Him or know Him. But you do know Him, because He remains with you and will be in you. I will not leave you as orphans; I am coming to you."

Never heard this before. Jesus is taking off, but sending some kind of spirit to take his place. A little weird because I don't think you can see a spirit, but cool that he's not just ditching his followers. – D

The Father, the Son, and the Holy Spirit

"In a little while the world will see Me no longer, but you will see Me. Because I live, you will live too. In that day you will know that I am in My Father, you are in Me, and I am in you. The one who has My commands and keeps them is the one who loves Me. And the one who loves Me will be loved by My Father. I also will love him and will reveal Myself to him."

He's into this whole me and the Father are one thing. Keeps saying it over and over. – D

*Hey PB, this is the whole trinity thing. God the Father, God the Son and God the Holy Spirit are all one. One God in three persons. I know it's hard to understand, but we aren't God and there are some things we will not be able to grasp. There is a verse in the Bible that says, "who can understand the mind of God?" And another verse that says, His ways are higher than our ways and His thoughts higher than our thoughts. I don't really fully understand the trinity either, but I believe it. I don't understand love, but I believe in it. I don't understand flight, but I see planes flying. Jesus is one with the Father.

- Uncle G.

Judas (not Iscariot) said to Him, "Lord, how is it You're going to reveal Yourself to us and not to the world?" Jesus answered, "If anyone loves Me, he will keep My word. My Father will love him, and We will come to him and make Our home with him. The one who doesn't love Me will not keep My words. The word that you hear is not Mine but is from the Father who sent Me. I have spoken these things to you while I remain with you. But the Counselor, the Holy Spirit—the Father will send Him in My name—will teach you all things and remind you of everything I have told you."* See my note on the next page.

How's that work? - PB

See my note on the next page.

Hmmm. I know a lot of people who claim to love God and don't seem to do what the Bible says is right. - V

Jesus' Gift of Peace

"Peace I leave with you. My peace I give to you. I do not give to you as the world gives. Your heart must not be troubled or fearful. You have heard Me tell you, 'I am going away and I am coming to you.' If you loved Me, you would have rejoiced that I am going to the Father, because the Father is greater than I. I have told you now before it happens so that when it does happen you may believe." ⟶ Pretty sure I'd believe if someone told me what was going to happen and it did. - PB

"I will not talk with you much longer, because the ruler of the world is coming. He has no power over Me. On the contrary, [I am going away] so that the world may know that I love the Father. Just as the Father commanded Me, so I do. Get up; let's leave this place."

CHAPTER 15

The Vine and the Branches

"I am the true vine, and My Father is the vineyard keeper. Every branch in Me that does not produce fruit He removes, and He prunes every branch that produces fruit so that it will produce more fruit. You are already clean

Apples? Oranges? Pears? - PB

*I remember one winter when I was about 8, Sheila (the neighbor girl) and I were at the little market on the corner. Her mom had given her 25 cents for candy. She wanted a big bag of hard candies so we could share, but it was 50 cents. Without thinking much about it, I grabbed the bag and shoved it inside my coat. As soon as I started to leave, I heard my mom's voice playing in my head. "Gideon Ronald Williams II, you make sure and represent that name with honor to make your Grandpa proud." Blood rushed to my head along with a heaping portion of guilt and I put the candy bag back on the shelf. I think that's how the Holy Spirit works in the lives of believers in Jesus. God puts the Holy Spirit inside of you when you decide to accept His forgiveness and believe in Jesus. Then the Holy Spirit kind of nudges, guides and directs you to do what pleases God - kind of like momma's voice in my head.

- Uncle G.

So, if fruit is the good stuff for God and people, then that's what proves a person is a believer in Jesus? If that's true, then believing in Jesus seems to be a bit more than just saying you believe - you must have to really believe in a way that changes your life. I like that much better than just saying, "Yeah, okay, sure I believe" and then nothing changes. Not sure I'm ready to go there yet, but I'd rather something like this totally change everything about me, than just be something I say. - D

The Life Book...Got Questions? Ask the person who gave you the life book or go to thelifebook.com because of the word I have spoken to you. Remain in Me, and I in you. Just as a branch is unable to produce fruit by itself unless it remains on the vine, so neither can you unless you <u>remain in Me</u>."

I think the fruit is the good stuff we do for God and others — like helping them come to believe in Jesus and showing them love when no one else loves them — stuff like that.
— Tay

"I am the vine; you are the branches. The one who remains in Me and I in him produces much fruit, because you can do nothing without Me. If anyone does not remain in Me, he is thrown aside like a branch and he withers. They gather them, throw them into the fire, and they ar<u>e burned.</u> If you remain in Me and My words remain in you, ask whatever you want and it will be done for you. My Father is glorified by this: that you produce much fruit and prove to be My (disciples.")

I want to stay attached to the vine.
— Tay

Christlike Love

"As the Father has loved Me, I have also loved you. Remain in My love. If you keep My commands you will remain in My love, just as I have kept My Father's commands and remain in His love. I have spoken these things to you so that My joy may be in you and your joy may be complete."

Having more joy in my life would be good. Most of the time I have the opposite. — V

"This is My command: love one another as I have loved you. No one has greater love than this, that someone would lay down his life for his friends. You are My friends if you do what I command you. I do not call you slaves anymore, because a slave doesn't know what his master is doing. I have called you <u>friends</u>, because I have made known to you everything I have heard from My Father."

AWESOME! Jesus is not just my savior and the son of God — he's also my friend.
— Tay

"You did not choose Me, but I chose you. I appointed you that you should go out and produce fruit and that your fruit should remain, so that whatever you ask the Father in My name, He will give you. This is what I command you: love one another."

Different definition of love than I'm used to. I've told my girl I love her, but not sure I'd die for her. (Hope she doesn't read this!) — PB

Persecutions Predicted

"If the world hates you, understand that it hated Me before it hated you. If you were of the world, the world would love [you as] its own. However, because you are not of the world, but I have chosen you out of it, the world hates you."

I can see the commercial now - "Follow Jesus and be hated". - D

"Remember the word I spoke to you: 'A slave is not greater than his master.' If they persecuted Me, they will also persecute you. If they kept My word, they will also keep yours. But they will do all these things to you on account of My name, because they don't know the One who sent Me."

"If I had not come and spoken to them, they would not have sin. Now they have no excuse for their sin. The one who hates Me also hates My Father. If I had not done the works among them that no one else has done, they would not have sin. Now they have seen and hated both Me and My Father. But [this happened] so that the statement written in their law might be fulfilled: They hated Me for no reason."

My younger brother is great at excuses and they always work to get him out of trouble. Yeah, I'm a bit jealous. - V

Coming Testimony and Rejection

"When the Counselor comes, the One I will send to you from the Father—the Spirit of truth who proceeds from the Father—He will testify about Me. You also will testify, because you have been with Me from the beginning."

CHAPTER 16

Can't imagine that happening today - banned from church. Probably wouldn't go over very well. - PB

"I have told you these things to keep you from stumbling. They will ban you from the synagogues. In fact, a time is coming when anyone who kills you will think he is offering service to God. They will do these things because they haven't known the Father or Me. But I have told you these things so that when their time comes you may remember I told them to you. I didn't tell you these things from the beginning, because I was with you."

The Counselor's Ministry

"But now I am going away to Him who sent Me, and not one of you asks Me, 'Where are You going?' Yet, because I have spoken these things to you, sorrow has filled your heart. Nevertheless, I am telling you the truth. It is for your benefit that I go away, because if I don't go away the Counselor will not come to you. If I go, I will send Him to you. "

I'd be bummed too if I left everything to follow him and now he's taking off. – D

"When He comes, He will convict the world about sin, righteousness, and judgment: about sin, because they do not believe in Me; about righteousness, because I am going to the Father and you will no longer see Me; and about judgment, because the ruler of this world has been judged. I still have many things to tell you, but you can't bear them now."

Job #2 of Holy Spirit: Make sure everyone knows they're on the hook for their sin? – PB

"When the Spirit of truth comes, He will guide you into all the truth. For He will not speak on His own, but He will speak whatever He hears. He will also declare to you what is to come. He will glorify Me, because He will take from what is Mine and declare it to you. Everything the Father has is Mine. This is why I told you that He takes from what is Mine and will declare it to you."

Sorrow Turned to Joy

"A little while and you will no longer see Me; again a little while and you will see Me." Therefore some of His disciples said to one another, "What is this He tells

I'm confused too. – V

us: 'A little while and you will not see Me; again a little while and you will see Me'; and, 'because I am going to the Father'?"

They said, "What is this He is saying, 'A little while'? We don't know what He's talking about!"

Jesus knew they wanted to question Him, so He said to them, "Are you asking one another about what I said, 'A little while and you will not see Me; again a little while and you will see Me'? I assure you: You will weep and wail, but the world will rejoice. You will become sorrowful, but your sorrow will turn to joy."

I think he's talking about when he is murdered on the cross. — Tay

"When a woman is in labor she has pain because her time has come. But when she has given birth to a child, she no longer remembers the suffering because of the joy that a person has been born into the world. So you also have sorrow now. But I will see you again. Your hearts will rejoice, and no one will rob you of your joy."

"In that day you will not ask Me anything. I assure you: Anything you ask the Father in My name, He will give you. Until now you have asked for nothing in My name. Ask and you will receive, that your joy may be complete."

Jesus the Victor

"I have spoken these things to you in figures of speech. A time is coming when I will no longer speak to you in figures, but I will tell you plainly about the Father. In that day you will ask in My name. I am not telling you that I will make requests to the Father on your behalf. For the Father Himself loves you, because you have loved Me and have believed that I came from God. I came from the Father and have come into the world. Again, I am leaving the world and going to the Father."

Repeats this thing a lot. – PB

"Ah!" His disciples said. "Now You're speaking plainly and not using any figurative language. Now we know that You know everything and don't need anyone to question You. By this we believe that You came from God."

Jesus responded to them, "Do you now believe? Look: An hour is coming, and has come, when each of you will be scattered to his own home, and you will leave Me alone. Yet I am not alone, because the Father is with Me. I have told you these things so that in Me you may have peace. You will have suffering in this world. Be courageous! I have conquered the world."

I think he's talking about when they run and hide after Jesus gets arrested. – Tay

CHAPTER 17

Jesus Prays for Himself
Jesus spoke these things, looked up to heaven, and said: Father, the hour has come. Glorify Your Son so that the Son may glorify You, for You gave Him authority over all flesh; so He may give eternal life to all You have given Him.

This is eternal life: that they may know You, the only true God, and the One You have sent—Jesus Christ.

Never thought of knowing God and Jesus Christ, as eternal life. In fact, didn't think much at all about knowing God before reading this and making comments. – PB

I have glorified You on the earth by completing the work You gave Me to do.
Now, Father, glorify Me in Your presence with that glory I had with You before
the world existed."

Jesus Prays for His Disciples

"I have revealed Your name to the men You gave Me from the world. They were
Yours, You gave them to Me, and they have kept Your word. Now they know
that all things You have given to Me are from You, because the words that
You gave Me, I have given them. They have received them and have known
for certain that I came from You. They have believed that You sent Me."

I think it's great that Jesus prays for his followers. - V

"I pray for them. I am not praying for the world but for those You have given Me,
because they are Yours. All My things are Yours, and Yours are Mine, and I have
been glorified in them. I am no longer in the world, but they are in the world,
and I am coming to You. Holy Father, protect them by Your name that You
have given Me, so that they may be one as We are one. While I was with them,
I was protecting them by Your name that You have given Me. I guarded them
and not one of them is lost, except the son of destruction, so that the Scripture
may be fulfilled."

Guessing the evil one is the devil. Not sure I want to follow Jesus yet, but I definitely don't want the devil messing with me. - D

Now I am coming to You, and I speak these things in the world so that
they may have My joy completed in them. I have given them Your word.
The world hated them because they are not of the world, as I am not
of the world. I am not praying that You take them out of the world but that
You protect them from the evil one. They are not of the world, as I am not
of the world. Sanctify them by the truth; Your word is truth. As You sent Me

into the world, I also have sent them into the world. I sanctify Myself for them, so they also may be sanctified by the truth."

Jesus Prays for All Believers

I pray not only for these, but also for those who believe in Me through their message. May they all be one, as You, Father, are in Me and I am in You. May they also be one in Us, so the world may believe You sent Me. I have given them the glory You have given Me. May they be one as We are one. I am in them and You are in Me. May they be made completely one, so the world may know You have sent Me and have loved them as You have loved Me.

Keeps talking about the whole being ONE thing. Over and over and over.
- PB

Father, I desire those You have given Me to be with Me where I am. Then they will see My glory, which You have given Me because You loved Me before the world's foundation. Righteous Father! The world has not known You. However, I have known You, and these have known that You sent Me. I made Your name known to them and will make it known, so the love You have loved Me with may be in them and I may be in them.

Hey Vanessa, in another part of the Bible it says that Jesus is now sitting by God the Father and praying for his followers all the time. So if you decide to become a believer in Jesus, you can be sure he'll be talking to God the Father about you all the time. That's an amazing thing when you think about it.

- Uncle G.

CHAPTER 18

Jesus Betrayed

After Jesus had said these things, He went out with His disciples across the Kidron Valley, where there was a garden, and He and His disciples went into it. Judas, who betrayed Him, also knew the place, because Jesus often met there with His disciples. So Judas took a company of soldiers and some temple police from the chief priests and the Pharisees and came there with lanterns, torches, and weapons.

Who needs enemies when you have friends like Judas - the ultimate frienemy? - V

Then Jesus, knowing everything that was about to happen to Him, went out and said to them, "Who is it you're looking for?" "Jesus the Nazarene," they answered. "I am He," Jesus told them.

→ Escaped every other time. - PB

Judas, who betrayed Him, was also standing with them. When He told them, "I am He," they stepped back and fell to the ground.

Were they afraid???? - Tay

Then He asked them again, "Who is it you're looking for?" "Jesus the Nazarene," they said. "I told you I am [He] ," Jesus replied. "So if you're looking for Me, let these men go." This was to fulfill the words He had said: "I have not lost one of those You have given Me."

→ OUCH! Peter goes crazy! - PB

Then Simon Peter, who had a sword, drew it, struck the high priest's slave, and cut off his right ear. (The slave's name was Malchus.) At that, Jesus said to Peter, "Sheathe your sword! Am I not to drink the cup the Father has given Me?"

I'm not sure why he calls it a cup, but he's talking about suffering and dying - paying the price for our sin to make us right with God. - Tay

Jesus Arrested and Taken to Annas

Then the company of soldiers, the commander, and the Jewish temple police arrested Jesus and tied Him up. First they led Him to Annas, for he was the father-in-law of Caiaphas, who was high priest that year. Caiaphas was the one who had advised the Jews that it was advantageous that one man should die for the people.

Peter Denies Jesus

Meanwhile Simon Peter was following Jesus, as was another disciple. That disciple was an acquaintance of the high priest; so he went with Jesus into the high priest's courtyard. But Peter remained standing outside by the door. So the other disciple, the one known to the high priest, went out and spoke to the girl who was the doorkeeper and brought Peter in.

Then the slave girl who was the doorkeeper said to Peter, "You aren't one of this man's disciples too, are you?" "I am not!" he said. Now the slaves and the temple police had made a charcoal fire, because it was cold. They were standing there warming themselves, and Peter was standing with them, warming himself.

#1 Denial - Didn't Peter say earlier that he'd die for Jesus? I've had a few friends ditch me too. Not fun. -D

Jesus before Annas

The high priest questioned Jesus about His disciples and about His teaching. "I have spoken openly to the world," Jesus answered him. "I have always taught in the synagogue and in the temple complex, where all the Jews congregate, and I haven't spoken anything in secret. Why do you question Me? Question those who heard what I told them. Look, they know what I said."

When He had said these things, one of the temple police standing by slapped Jesus, saying, "Is this the way you answer the high priest?" "If I have spoken wrongly," Jesus answered him, "give evidence about the wrong; but if rightly, why do you hit Me?" Then Annas sent Him bound to Caiaphas the high priest.

Really? They slapped him! Weird. - PB

Guess he didn't know what to say. - D

Peter Denies Jesus Twice More

#2 Denial - D

Now Simon Peter was standing and warming himself. They said to him, "You aren't one of His disciples too, are you?" He denied it and said, "I am not!" One of the high priest's slaves, a relative of the man whose ear Peter had cut off, said, "Didn't I see you with Him in the garden?" Peter then denied it again. Immediately a rooster crowed.

#3 Denial - BAM Jesus nailed it. - D

Jesus before Pilate

Then they took Jesus from Caiaphas to the governor's headquarters. It was early morning. They did not enter the headquarters themselves; otherwise they would be defiled and unable to eat the Passover. Then Pilate came out to them and said, "What charge do you bring against this man?" They answered him, "If this man weren't a criminal, we wouldn't have handed Him over to you."

So Pilate told them, "Take Him yourselves and judge Him according to your law." "It's not legal for us to put anyone to death," the Jews declared. They said this so that Jesus' words might be fulfilled signifying what sort of death He was going to die.

Can you please kill him for us? Nice guys - D

Then Pilate went back into the headquarters, summoned Jesus, and said to Him, "Are You the King of the Jews?" Jesus answered, "Are you asking this on your own, or have others told you about Me?"

"I'm not a Jew, am I?" Pilate replied. "Your own nation and the chief priests handed You over to me. What have You done?"

"My kingdom is not of this world," said Jesus. "If My kingdom were of this world, My servants would fight, so that I wouldn't be handed over to the Jews. As it is, My kingdom does not have its origin here."

So is Jesus against fighting? - V

"You are a king then?" Pilate asked. "You say that I'm a king," Jesus replied. "I was born for this, and I have come into the world for this: to testify to the truth. Everyone who is of the truth listens to My voice."

"What is truth?" said Pilate.

I think this is the hardest part for my dad believing that Jesus is THE truth and not just one out of a whole bunch of religions that are true. I'm still praying for him. - Tay

Jesus or Barabbas
After he had said this, he went out to the Jews again and told them, "I find no grounds for charging Him. You have a custom that I release one [prisoner] to you at the Passover. So, do you want me to release to you the King of the Jews?" They shouted back, "Not this man, but Barabbas!" Now Barabbas was a revolutionary.

Pilate doesn't seem to want to kill him. - D

Sure seems like the people want him dead! Quick change from cheering him to killing him. Remind me never to be popular like that. - PB

CHAPTER 19

Jesus Flogged and Mocked

Goes from letting him off to pounding on him. - PB

Then Pilate took Jesus and had Him flogged. The soldiers also twisted together a crown of thorns, put it on His head, and threw a purple robe around Him. And they repeatedly came up to Him and said, "Hail, King of the Jews!" and were slapping His face. Pilate went outside again and said to them, "Look, I'm bringing Him outside to you to let you know I find no grounds for charging Him."

okay. so he has him beaten and then says he's done nothing wrong. What kind of justice is that? - V

Pilate Sentences Jesus to Death

Then Jesus came out wearing the crown of thorns and the purple robe. Pilate said to them, "Here is the man!" When the chief priests and the temple police saw Him, they shouted, "Crucify! Crucify!"

Pilate responded, "Take Him and crucify Him yourselves, for I find no grounds for charging Him." → *Still trying to get off easy. - PB*

That's strange. Why would such a powerful guy be afraid, unless he thought it might be true? - D

"We have a law," the Jews replied to him, "and according to that law He must die, because He made Himself the Son of God." When Pilate heard this statement, he was more afraid than ever. He went back into the headquarters and asked Jesus, "Where are You from?" But Jesus did not give him an answer.

So Pilate said to Him, "You're not talking to me? Don't You know that I have the authority to release You and the authority to crucify You?" "You would have no authority over Me at all," Jesus answered him, "if it hadn't been given you from above. This is why the one who handed Me over to you has the greater sin."

Hey man! You should be begging me for your life! - PB

Jesus is the King of all Kings! - Tay

From that moment Pilate made every effort to release Him. But the Jews shouted, "If you release this man, you are not Caesar's friend. Anyone who makes himself a king opposes Caesar!"

When Pilate heard these words, he brought Jesus outside. He sat down on the judge's bench in a place called the Stone Pavement (but in Hebrew Gabbatha). It was the preparation day for the Passover, and it was about six in the morning. Then he told the Jews, "Here is your king!" But they shouted, "Take Him away! Take Him away! Crucify Him!"

I didn't know Pilate tried so hard not to kill Jesus. – V ♡

Pilate said to them, "Should I crucify your king?" "We have no king but Caesar!" the chief priests answered. So then, because of them, he handed Him over to be crucified.

The Crucifixion

Wonder how heavy that thing was? – PB

Therefore they took Jesus away. Carrying His own cross, He went out to what is called Skull Place, which in Hebrew is called Golgotha. There they crucified Him and two others with Him, one on either side, with Jesus in the middle. Pilate also had a sign lettered and put on the cross. The inscription was: JESUS THE NAZARENE THE KING OF THE JEWS

Many of the Jews read this sign, because the place where Jesus was crucified was near the city, and it was written in Hebrew, Latin, and Greek. So the chief priests of the Jews said to Pilate, "Don't write, 'The King of the Jews,' but that He said, 'I am the King of the Jews.'" Pilate replied, "What I have written, I have written."

I'm thinking Pilate believed Jesus was at least someone special. – D

When the soldiers crucified Jesus, they took His clothes and divided them into four parts, a part for each soldier. They also took the tunic, which was seamless, woven in one piece from the top. So they said to one another, "Let's not tear it, but toss for it, to see who gets it." [They did this] to fulfill the <u>Scripture</u> that says: They divided My clothes among themselves, and they cast lots for My clothing. And this is what the soldiers did.

This is just one of the prophecies I learned about that Jesus fulfilled. It's pretty amazing when you check it out. — Tay

Jesus' Provision for His Mother

Standing by the cross of Jesus were His mother, His mother's sister, Mary the wife of Clopas, and Mary Magdalene. When Jesus saw His mother and the disciple He loved standing there, He said to His mother, "Woman, here is your son." Then He said to the disciple, "Here is your mother." And from that hour the disciple took her into his home.

→ Taking care of mom. Nice touch. — PB

The Finished Work of Jesus

After this, when Jesus knew that everything was now accomplished that the Scripture might be fulfilled, He said, "I'm thirsty!" A jar full of sour wine was sitting there; so they fixed a sponge full of sour wine on hyssop and held it up to His mouth. When Jesus had received the sour wine, He said, "It is finished!" Then bowing His head, He gave up His spirit.

What is finished? — D

Jesus' Side Pierced

Since it was the preparation day, the Jews did not want the bodies to remain on the cross on the Sabbath (for that Sabbath was a special day). They requested that Pilate have the men's legs broken and that [their bodies] be taken away. So the soldiers came and broke the legs of the first man and of the other one who had been crucified with Him. When they came to Jesus, they did not break His legs since they saw that He was already dead. But one of the soldiers pierced His side with a spear, and at once blood and water came out. He who saw this has testified so that you also may believe. His testimony is true, and he knows he is telling the truth. For these things happened so that the Scripture would <u>be fulfilled:</u> Not one of His bones will be broken. Also, another Scripture says: They will look at the One they pierced.

There it is again, another prophecy fulfilled.
— Tay

* I once had a friend that did some time as a teen for stealing a car. From the time he was arrested to the time he got out of lock up seemed like forever. He got out right before his eighteenth birthday. I remember because the judge expunged his record on his birthday. That means it was like he'd never committed the crime. It was finished and his record was clean. When Jesus dies on the cross, he's not just dying like a normal person. He's paying the price for our sin. When he says, "it is finished," he's saying he did what God sent him to do and the final part of that was his death to finally break the curse of sin. The curse is now broken — it is finished — and each of us can now have our sins forgiven.

— Uncle G.

Jesus' Burial

After this, Joseph of Arimathea, who was a disciple of Jesus—but secretly because of his fear of the Jews—asked Pilate that he might remove Jesus' body. Pilate gave him permission, so he came and took His body away.

Nicodemus (who had previously come to Him at night) also came, bringing a mixture of about 75 pounds of myrrh and aloes. Then they took Jesus' body and wrapped it in linen cloths with the aromatic spices, according to the burial custom of the Jews. There was a garden in the place where He was crucified. A new tomb was in the garden; no one had yet been placed in it. They placed Jesus there because of the Jewish preparation and since the tomb was nearby.

That's a ton! - PB

CHAPTER 20

*Kind of weird - Hey, here's an open tomb, let's use that one! - Uncle G.

The Empty Tomb

On the first day of the week Mary Magdalene came to the tomb early, while it was still dark. She saw that the stone had been removed from the tomb. So she ran to Simon Peter and to the other disciple, the one Jesus loved, and said to them, "They have taken the Lord out of the tomb, and we don't know where they have put Him!" At that, Peter and the other disciple went out, heading for the tomb.

Possible Body Snatchers! - PB

The two were running together, but the other disciple outran Peter and got to the tomb first. Stooping down, he saw the linen cloths lying there, yet he did not go in. Then, following him, Simon Peter came also. He entered the tomb and saw the linen cloths lying there. The wrapping that had been on His head was not lying with the linen cloths but was folded up in a separate place by itself.

The other disciple, who had reached the tomb first, then entered the tomb, saw, and believed. For they still did not understand the Scripture that He must rise from the dead. Then the disciples went home again.

Mary Magdalene Sees the Risen Lord

But Mary stood outside facing the tomb, crying. As she was crying, she stooped to look into the tomb. She saw two angels in white sitting there, one at the head and one at the feet, where Jesus' body had been lying.

They said to her, "Woman, why are you crying?" "Because they've taken away my Lord," she told them, "and I don't know where they've put Him." Having said this, she turned around and saw Jesus standing there, though she did not know it was Jesus.

"Woman," Jesus said to her, "why are you crying? Who is it you are looking for?" Supposing He was the gardener, she replied, "Sir, if you've removed Him, tell me where you've put Him, and I will take Him away." Jesus said, "Mary." Turning around, she said to Him in Hebrew, "Rabbouni!" — which means "Teacher."

"Don't cling to Me," Jesus told her, "for I have not yet ascended to the Father. But go to My brothers and tell them that I am ascending to My Father and your

Father—to My God and your God." Mary Magdalene went and announced to the disciples, "I have seen the Lord!" And she told them what He had said to her.

Did they believe her or think she'd lost it? - D

The Disciples Commissioned

In the evening of that first day of the week, the disciples were [gathered together] with the doors locked because of their fear of the Jews. Then Jesus came, stood among them, and said to them, "Peace to you!" Having said this, He showed them His hands and His side.

So, did he just like poof through the door? - D

So the disciples rejoiced when they saw the Lord. Jesus said to them again, "Peace to you! As the Father has sent Me, I also send you." After saying this, He breathed on them and said, "Receive the Holy Spirit. If you forgive the sins of any, they are forgiven them; if you retain [the sins of] any, they are retained."

Did he have bad breath from being dead? - PB

Seems like a little too much power to give a person. - D

Thomas Sees and Believes

But one of the Twelve, Thomas (called "Twin"), was not with them when Jesus came. So the other disciples kept telling him, "We have seen the Lord!" But he said to them, "If I don't see the mark of the nails in His hands, put my finger into the mark of the nails, and put my hand into His side, I will never believe!"

Same thing I would've said. - D

After eight days His disciples were indoors again, and Thomas was with them. Even though the doors were locked, Jesus came and stood among them.

Rises from the dead and goes through doors! Massive skills! - PB

He said, "Peace to you!" Then He said to Thomas, "Put your finger here and observe My hands. Reach out your hand and put it into My side. Don't be an unbeliever, but a believer." Thomas responded to Him, "My Lord and my God!" Jesus said, "Because you have seen Me, you have believed. Those who believe without seeing are <u>blessed</u>."

I think that's me. I believe. — Tay

The Purpose of This Gospel

Jesus performed many other signs in the presence of His disciples that are not written in this book. But these are written so that you may believe Jesus is the Messiah, the Son of God, and by believing you may have life in His <u>name.</u>

I hope everyone reading this book decides to believe in Jesus and gets to have eternal life just like it says here. — Tay

CHAPTER 21

Jesus' Third Appearance to the Disciples

After this, Jesus revealed Himself again to His disciples by the Sea of Tiberias. He revealed Himself in this way: Simon Peter, Thomas (called "Twin"), Nathanael from Cana of Galilee, Zebedee's sons, and two others of His disciples were together.

"I'm going fishing," Simon Peter said to them. "We're coming with you," they told him. They went out and got into the boat, but that night they caught nothing.

My grandpa would've caught something. He always catches fish when I go with him — V

When daybreak came, Jesus stood on the shore. However, the disciples did not know it was Jesus. "Men," Jesus called to them, "you don't have any fish, do you?" "No," they answered.

"Cast the net on the right side of the boat," He told them, "and you'll find some." So they did, and they were unable to haul it in because of the large number of fish.

Can I take this guy fishing with me? - D

It seems weird to put clothes on to jump in the water. - V

Therefore the disciple, the one Jesus loved, said to Peter, "It is the Lord!" When Simon Peter heard that it was the Lord, he tied his outer garment around him (for he was stripped) and plunged into the sea. But since they were not far from land (about 100 yards away), the other disciples came in the boat, dragging the net full of fish. When they got out on land, they saw a charcoal fire there, with fish lying on it, and bread.

"Bring some of the fish you've just caught," Jesus told them. So Simon Peter got up and hauled the net ashore, full of large fish—153 of them. Even though there were so many, the net was not torn. "Come and have breakfast," Jesus told them.

I think this is so amazing. Jesus was just killed, came back from the dead and is now making breakfast for his followers. The son of God making breakfast. Wow! - Tay

None of the disciples dared ask Him, "Who are You?" because they knew it was the Lord. Jesus came, took the bread, and gave it to them. He did the same with the fish. This was now the third time Jesus appeared to the disciples after He was raised from the dead.

Jesus' Threefold Restoration of Peter
When they had eaten breakfast, Jesus asked Simon Peter, "Simon, son of John, do you love Me more than these?"

Good question after he denied him a few days ago. - D

"Yes, Lord," he said to Him, "You know that I love You." "Feed My lambs," He told him.

A second time He asked him, "Simon, son of John, do you love Me?" "Yes, Lord," he said to Him, "You know that I love You." "Shepherd My sheep," He told him.

He asked him the third time, "Simon, son of John, do you love Me?" Peter was grieved that He asked him the third time, "Do you love Me?" He said, "Lord, You know everything! You know that I love You." "Feed My sheep,"

I get it — denied him 3 times — has to say he loves him 3 times. – PB

reading Jesus' story like this kind of opened my eyes. He's easy to love. – V

Jesus said. "I assure you: When you were young, you would tie your belt and walk wherever you wanted. But when you grow old, you will stretch out your hands and someone else will tie you and carry you where you don't want to go." He said this to signify by what kind of death he would glorify God. After saying this, He told him, "Follow Me!"

Not complicated. I think I'm pretty much ready to follow him. – D

Correcting a False Report
So Peter turned around and saw the disciple Jesus loved following them. [That disciple] was the one who had leaned back against Jesus at the supper and asked, "Lord, who is the one that's going to betray You?"

When Peter saw him, he said to Jesus, "Lord—what about him?" "If I want him to remain until I come," Jesus answered, "what is that to you? As for you, follow

Me." So this report spread to the brothers that this disciple would not die. Yet Jesus did not tell him that he would not die, but, "If I want him to remain until I come, what is that to you?"

I love that. Jesus says "what is that to you? That is very cool. – V

Epilogue

This is the disciple who testifies to these things and who wrote them down. We know that his testimony is true. And there are also many other things that Jesus did, which, if they were written one by one, I suppose not even the world itself could contain the books that would be <u>written.</u>

I'd like to read them.
— Tay

WHAT ABOUT YOU?

NOW IS YOUR CHANCE TO MAKE A <u>CRUCIAL DECISION</u> ABOUT YOUR LIFE AND YOUR FUTURE.

Best decision I've ever made!
– Tay

Jesus asked an important question when He was here on Earth:

"Who do YOU say that I am?"

WHO DO YOU SAY JESUS IS?

Is He the son of God? Did He live without sin? Did He pay the penalty for Your sin, breaking the curse? Did He rise again from the dead?

He was either crazy to die when He could have easily avoided it or He was and is the son of God.

Who do You say Jesus is?
   a. Son of God who lived a sinless life and died to pay for my sin
   b. Crazy peasant preacher who died for nothing
   c. _____

The next most important question is:

WHO ARE YOU?

Are you a sinner who has inherited the curse placed on all people? Is your sin keeping you from God? What is your eternal destination, heaven or hell?

The Bible says in John 3:18 that if you don't believe in who Jesus is and what He has done for you, then right now you stand condemned to an eternity in hell.

Who are you?

a. Under the curse, condemned to hell without Jesus
b. Doing fine without God and not worried about when I die
c. _____

SO, WHAT WILL YOU DO?

Jesus Said ,"Come Follow Me."

If you agree with God, (confess) that you are a sinner who desperately needs your sins paid for with the ultimate sacrifice, there is good news.

In the Bible, in the book of 1 John, God says: "If you confess your sins, He is faithful and just to forgive you."

God can forgive you based on the sacrifice of Jesus.

In the Bible, in the book of Romans God says:

"If you confess with your mouth Jesus is Lord and believe in your heart that God raised Him from the dead, you will be saved."

It doesn't matter who you are or what you've done. You don't have to clean up your life first. God is passionately in love with you and is waiting with open arms for you to run to him. You can make that decision right now, wherever you are and whatever you're doing.

How to Make Things Right With God (and get to Heaven)

1. Confess to God you are a sinner.
   ☐ SAY "God, I admit I'm a sinner"

2. Tell Him you believe Jesus died to pay the penalty for your sin and rose from the dead to give you new life.
   ☐ SAY "I believe Jesus' death on the cross paid the penalty for my sin and his rising from the dead gives me new life"

3. Tell Him that you trust Jesus to forgive you and give you a fresh start.
   ☐ SAY "God, I trust you to forgive my sins and give me a fresh start"

4. Ask Him to come and live in you through His spirit.
   ☐ SAY "God, please come and live in me by your Holy Spirit"

5. Commit your life to following Him and His ways.
   ☐ SAY "I commit my life to follow Your ways, not my ways. Please help me do that. Amen."

Okay, so when I started reading and making notes, I thought it would just be fun. Now, I'm pretty much ready to say I believe. I need forgiveness and want to follow Jesus. Crazy. - D

Sometimes this isn't easy. It means your life has to change from doing things the way you've always done them to doing them more like Jesus would do them. Things like showing love when you just want to punch someone or talk trash about them. Choosing to do what's right even when everyone else is doing what's wrong (that can be lonely. Trust me.) putting others' needs before your needs that one is very tough for me. I'm kind of selfish. The good news is the Holy Spirit now lives inside of you (sounds kind of freaky when you think about it) and He helps you to follow Jesus. - Tay

If you decided to follow Jesus today, the Bible says your name is now written in the Lamb's Book of Life.

Sign your name below with today's date so you can remember the day you decided to follow Jesus.

_____   _____

Child of God/Follower of Jesus (Your Name)   Today's Date

All these years of going to church, and I've never actually
prayed a prayer to have my sins forgiven and commit to
being a follower of Jesus. Today is my day.

– V

FIRST STEPS

- Contact the person who gave you the Life Book and let them know of your decision. They will be very happy for you!

- Ask the person who gave you the Life Book to help you get a complete Bible to read.

- Go to church with the person who gave you the Life Book or find a church in your area at thelifebook.com to help you in your new life of following Jesus.

- Read a little bit of your Bible every day.

- Talk to God every day. Let him know your concerns, your worries, and ask for His help and direction in your new life.

- Find friends who follow Jesus.

- Tell others about your new decision to follow Jesus Christ.

HELP!

THIS SECTION IS FOR EVERYONE WHO HAS EVER WISHED THEY COULD SIT DOWN WITH GOD AND ASK HIM ABOUT PROBLEMS IN THEIR LIFE. YOU MAY NOT BE STRUGGLING RIGHT NOW, BUT MAYBE A FRIEND NEEDS YOUR HELP. WE HAVE PROVIDED SOME PASSAGES FROM THE BIBLE THAT WILL HOPEFULLY HELP YOU THROUGH AND GIVE YOU SOME GUIDANCE.

RELATIONSHIPS AND SEX

Am I really in love?

Love is patient; love is kind. Love does not envy; is not boastful; is not conceited; does not act improperly; is not selfish; is not provoked; does not keep a record of wrongs; finds no joy in unrighteousness, but rejoices in the truth; bears all things, believes all things, hopes all things, endures all things. (1 Corinthians 13:4-7)

I haven't really met many guys who look at love this way. Most of the guys around here are totally selfish, and all most of them do is brag about how great they are. So is that really love? Maybe not! —V

Sex...Am I ready for it?

Guard your heart above all else, for it is the source of life. (Proverbs 4:23)

Do you not know that if you offer yourselves to someone as obedient <u>slaves</u>, you are <u>slaves</u> of that one you obey—either of sin leading to death or of obedience leading to righteousness? (Romans 6:16)

For this is God's will, your sanctification: that you abstain from sexual immorality, so that each of you knows how to possess his own vessel in sanctification and honor, not with lustful desires, like the Gentiles who don't know God. (1 Thessalonians 4:3-5)

What is all this talk about slaves and sanctification? Are we still talking about sex? —PB

So many of my friends think they are ready for sex. But what do we really know? Are we ready for babies, for STD's, and for broken hearts? I have a really good friend who thought she and her boyfriend were ready for sex, so they went ahead and had it. She thought it was love, but found out pretty fast that it wasn't. She gave up her heart to a guy who didn't really care, and dumped her a few weeks later. But then she figured that since she had already had sex once, it wasn't a big deal to do it again... and again...and again. That is what being a "slave" means — she couldn't stop herself, even though she hated herself more and more every time she had sex with another guy. Are you really ready for all that sex brings with it? — Tay

How far is too far? *

Flee from sexual immorality! "Every sin a person can commit is outside the body," but the person who is sexually immoral sins against his own body. (1 Corinthians 6:18)

*Kids always ask me how far is too far. I tell them that even thinking about sex is too far. I was a teenage boy once and I know how their minds work. You think you can stop with just kissing, but then you go to the next step. Before long, you've already had sex, and you don't even remember making a choice to go that far - it just happened. Don't even let your mind go there, and then the next step never comes at you. God's plan is for you to wait until you're married.

-Uncle G.

But sexual immorality and any impurity or greed should not even be heard of among you, as is proper for saints. (Ephesians 5:3)

Don't lust in your heart for her beauty or let her captivate you with her eyelashes. (Proverb 6:25)

But I tell you, everyone who looks at a woman to lust for her has already committed adultery with her in his heart. (Matthew 5:28)

I've had sex, now I feel guilty...
Therefore if anyone is in Christ, there is a new creation; old things have passed away, and look, new things have come. (II Corinthians 5:17)

If we confess our sins, He is faithful and righteous to forgive us our sins and to cleanse us from all unrighteousness. (I John 1:9)

It's good to know that even when we've messed up, God gives us a clean slate.
– V

Wait a minute – if I even think about doing stuff with a girl, its the same as if I already did it? That's not right! I'm a gamer – I understand the difference between reality and fantasy. If the game I'm playing is about killing people, it doesn't mean I've really killed anyone – it's NOT REAL! So how is thinking about sex like having sex?
–D

FRIENDS / PEER PRESSURE

Therefore, submit to God. But resist the Devil, and he will flee from you. (James 4:7)

No temptation has overtaken you except what is common to humanity. God is faithful and He will not allow you to be tempted beyond what you are able, but with the temptation He will also provide a way of escape, so that you are able to bear it. (1 Corinthian 10:13)

Do not be deceived: "Bad company corrupts good morals." Become right-minded and stop sinning, because some people are ignorant about God. (1 Corinthians 15:33-34)

You must not follow a crowd in wrongdoing. Do not testify in a lawsuit and go along with a crowd to pervert [justice]. Do not show favoritism to a poor person in his lawsuit. (Exodus 23:2-3)

Don't set foot on the path of the wicked; don't proceed in the way of evil ones. Avoid it; don't travel on it. Turn away from it, and pass it by. For they can't sleep unless they have done what is evil; they are robbed of sleep unless they make someone stumble. (Proverbs 4:14-16)

But when Herod's birthday celebration came, Herodias' daughter danced before them and pleased Herod. So he promised with an oath to give her whatever she might ask. And prompted by her mother, she answered, "Give me

John the Baptist's head here on a platter!" Although the king regretted it, he commanded that it be granted because of his oaths and his guests. So he sent orders and had John beheaded in the prison. (Matthew 14:6-10)

But they kept up the pressure, demanding with loud voices that He be crucified. And their voices won out. So Pilate decided to grant their demand. (Luke 23:23-24)

I kind of realized something the other day after watching how my friends act. All they care about is what other people think. I hate to admit it, but I guess I'm kind of like them. It's like I let everyone else's opinion run my life. Doesn't really make any sense now that I think about it. It's still hard. But I'm thinking about finding some different friends that pressure me to do good stuff instead of bad stuff. Not sure if that's the answer, but I think it'll help.
—PB

My dad always says "Misery loves company"— people who pressure you into doing bad things are usually just looking for someone to share the blame or get down in the dirt with them!
— Tay

SELF IMAGE / SELF-ESTEEM

<u>I will praise</u> You, because I have been remarkably and wonderfully made. Your works are wonderful, and I know [this] very well. My bones were not hidden from You when I was made in secret, when I was formed in the depths of the earth. Your eyes saw me when I was formless; all [my] days were written in Your book and planned before a single one of them began. (Psalm 139:14-16)

Therefore we do not give up; even though our outer person is being destroyed, our inner person is being renewed day by day. (2 Corinthians 4:16)

Do you not know that your body is a sanctuary of the Holy Spirit, who is in you, whom you have from God? You are not your own, for you were bought at a price; therefore glorify God in your body. (1Corinthians 6:19-20)

Therefore, brothers, by the mercies of God, I urge you to present your bodies as a living sacrifice, holy and pleasing to God; this is your spiritual worship. (Romans 12:1)

But the LORD said to Samuel, "Do not look at his appearance or his stature, because I have rejected him. Man does not see what the LORD sees, for man sees what is visible, but the LORD sees the heart. (1 Samuel 16:7)

He gives greater grace. Therefore He says: God resists the proud, but gives grace to the humble. (James 4:6)

"Whoever welcomes this little child in My name welcomes Me. And whoever welcomes Me welcomes Him who sent Me. For whoever is least among you—this one is great." (Luke 9:48)

My friends face so many issues that all come back to self-image. Steroids, eating disorders, crazy diets, cutting, arrogance, bullying...the list goes on. I wish everyone would see that God made each one of us special and just accept who they really are. — Tay

I always used to think I was fat. When I was in 6th grade, I used to make myself throw up all the time to help lose weight. The youth leader at my church found me in the bathroom one day and talked to me about how God thinks I'm beautiful and my body is like His temple or something He is really proud of. She told me to focus on being beautiful on the inside. It sounded cheesy, but after a few years, I started to see that I wasn't fat, and in fact, God had done a pretty good job when He made me!
—V

DEPRESSION / WORRY

Why am I so depressed? Why this turmoil within me? Put your hope in God, for I will still praise Him, my Savior and my God. (Psalm 42:5)

Trust in the LORD with all your heart, and do not rely on your own understanding; think about Him in all your ways, and He will guide you on the right paths. (Proverbs 3:5-6)

Now may the God of hope fill you with all joy and peace in believing, so that you may overflow with hope by the power of the Holy Spirit. (Romans 15:13)

Rejoice in the Lord always. I will say it again: Rejoice! Let your graciousness be known to everyone. The Lord is near. Don't worry about anything, but in everything, through prayer and petition with thanksgiving; let your requests be made known to God. And the peace of God, which surpasses every thought, will guard your hearts and your minds in Christ Jesus. (Philippians 4:4-7)

We are pressured in every way but not crushed; we are perplexed but not in despair; we are persecuted but not abandoned; we are struck down but not destroyed. Therefore we do not give up; even though our outer person is being destroyed, our inner person is being renewed day by day. (2 Corinthians 4:8-9, 16)

But those who trust in the LORD will renew their strength; they will soar on wings like eagles; they will run and not grow weary; they will walk and not faint. (Isaiah 40:31)

So people in the bible were depressed too?
Good to know I'm not the only one!
 - V

I have trouble with this. I trust God, really I do. But it's so hard to not worry about things. My mom is amazing with this. She has faced some really hard times in her life, but she is always so peaceful and doesn't stress out about it. I know she prays all the time and tells anyone who will listen to her that God has been good to her. It's just amazing to me that she can be so positive at times when everyone else falls into massive depression.
 - Tay

I don't know that I would say I've ever been "depressed." There are times I feel really overwhelmed and don't want to think about things anymore - that's when I go online and play video games even more than I do now. There are times in life when I just get so tired of dealing with garbage, so I like this verse - it would be cool to fly like a bird - high above all the problems in this world.
 - D

MY NOTES

"...keep in mind the words of the Lord Jesus, for He said, 'It is more **blessed** to **give** than to **receive**.'"

Acts 20:35

WHO WILL YOU GIVE
THE LIFE BOOK TO?

thelifebook.com

facebook.com/thelifebookmovement

GOT QUESTIONS?

Go to thelifebook.com

WANT A COPY OF THE LIFE BOOK FOR YOUR FRIENDS?

FREE and downloadable in different formats...Go to thelifebook.com

WANT TO BRING THE LIFE BOOK CAMPAIGN TO YOUR AREA?

Go to thelifebook.com

SHARE YOUR STORY

facebook.com/thelifebookmovement